D0330981

BACK PORCH
·FAITH·

To Steve —
 With my best wishes.
             Thanks,
                 Paul Prather
                 10/23/99

OTHER BOOKS BY PAUL PRATHER

Modern-Day Miracles

Life's a Dance: The Story of John Michael Montgomery

BACK PORCH
• F A I T H •
Weekly Meditations

PAUL PRATHER

**Andrews McMeel
Publishing**

Kansas City

www.andrewsmcmeel.com

99 00 01 02 03 RDC 10 9 8 7 6 5 4 3 2 1

Library of Congress Cataloging-in-Publication Data

Prather, Paul.
Back porch faith : weekly meditations / by Paul Prather.
p. cm.
ISBN 0-7407-0047-2
1. Meditations.   2. Devotional calendars.   I. Title.
BV4832.2.P65 1999
242'.2—dc21   99-15624
CIP

Design and composition by Mauna Eichner

Some essays in this book appeared in earlier forms in the *Lexington Herald-Leader*. They are reprinted with permission.

ATTENTION: SCHOOLS AND BUSINESSES

Andrews McMeel books are available at quantity discounts with bulk purchase for educational, business, or sales promotional use. For information, please write to: Special Sales Department, Andrews McMeel Publishing, 4520 Main Street, Kansas City, Missouri 64111.

THIS BOOK IS FOR MY SON,
JOHN PRATHER

CONTENTS

INTRODUCTION   xi

Week 1   THE WORLD OPERATES ON
SPIRITUAL LAWS, TOO   1

Week 2   TIME'S HEADLIGHTS   6

Week 3   IT'S NEVER TOO LATE TO FORGIVE   11

Week 4   THE POWER OF PRAYER IS A COMFORT   16

Week 5   WHEN GOD SEEMS CAPRICIOUS   21

Week 6   MORE ON SPIRITUAL LAWS   26

Week 7   THE LAW OF SOWING AND REAPING   31

Week 8   DESIRE MAKES A DIFFERENCE   35

Week 9   "WANT-TO" ONLY GOES SO FAR   40

Week 10   THE TEN RULES   44

Week 11   WE HONOR GOD'S NAME, OURSELVES,
OUR PARENTS   49

Week 12	THE HEART OF A KILLER	54
Week 13	THE REMAINING RULES OF LOVE	59
Week 14	THE MAJESTIC STORY OF PASSOVER	64
Week 15	RESURRECTION MERCY	69
Week 16	MEETING HEAVEN'S WELCOMING COMMITTEE	74
Week 17	WHAT IS HELL LIKE?	79
Week 18	CHURCH IS INDEED A PLACE FOR HYPOCRITES	83
Week 19	WHY DO RELIGIONS MAKE THOSE NETTLING LAWS?	88
Week 20	A GREAT DETERMINED WOMAN	93
Week 21	HOW TO ENJOY A HAPPY MARRIAGE	98
Week 22	A COVENANT IS WHY WE STAY	103
Week 23	WE ALL NEED A BACK PORCH TO ESCAPE LIFE'S STORMS	108
Week 24	CHEERFUL GIVERS	112
Week 25	TAKE HEART, YOU LOSERS	117
Week 26	KENTUCKY'S "KING" SOLOMON	121

Week 27   ON SOFTBALL, AGE, AND ACCEPTANCE   126

Week 28   WHAT MY MOTHER'S INNER PEACE
TAUGHT ME   130

Week 29   WE'RE SHAPED BY PREDESTINATION
AND FREE WILL   134

Week 30   JESUS, THE MODEL LEADER   138

Week 31   JESUS WOULD HAVE MADE YOU MAD   143

Week 32   JESUS SPOKE FAITH-FILLED WORDS   148

Week 33   LIFE MULTIPLIES FROM DEATH   153

Week 34   FATHERHOOD IS EQUAL PARTS
LOVE AND PAIN   158

Week 35   MY SON TAKES HIS TURN AT BAT   162

Week 36   THE HIGH COST OF TRUTH   168

Week 37   MINISTERS ARE ONLY HUMAN   174

Week 38   CHAIN OF COMMAND   180

Week 39   WE REDISCOVER PRAYER DURING
TROUBLED TIMES   184

Week 40   PEOPLE NEED A LITTLE PRAISE   189

Week 41   PROPHETS WITHOUT HONOR   193

Week 42   HALLOWEENS VERSUS HALLELUJAHS   198

Week 43   LOW CHURCH RELIGION GETS A
BAD RAP   203

Week 44   MY "LOST WEEKEND" GETS FOUND   208

Week 45   WE TRUST IN SATELLITES' BEAMS
AND E-MAILS   213

Week 46   GOD'S FAVOR CAN OPEN DOORS   218

Week 47   THIS IS THE SEASON TO COUNT
YOUR BLESSINGS   223

Week 48   HE CARES ABOUT THE NEUROTIC   228

Week 49   THE WALL BETWEEN LIFE AND
DEATH IS THIN   232

Week 50   RELIGIOUS REVIVALS OFFER HOPE
FOR OUR WORLD   237

Week 51   WE SHOULD REMEMBER GRACE   242

Week 52   A REMEMBRANCE OF A
SMALL BOY'S HERO   247

INTRODUCTION

You'll find within the pages of this book that life—which is another way of saying God—has taken me on some paradoxical journeys. Most of those trips I've neither planned nor anticipated, and this book is as much as anything a result of my desire to sort out the causes, meanings, and results of those experiences.

For instance, I grew up in a succession of obscure Kentucky towns, the son of an itinerant Baptist minister. We rarely had any money. By the time I was a teenager the two things I desired most were a permanent place to live and an abundance of cash and prestige.

So I made up my mind to become a lawyer. I intended to graduate from college and law school and then return to Campbellsville, my favorite of the towns in which we'd lived. There I'd build a prosperous, quiet practice. Basically I hoped to become *To Kill a Mockingbird*'s Atticus Finch, but without the inbred likes of Bob Ewell stalking me.

I wanted as little as possible to do with religion, which I saw as at best a bore and at worst a sop for the dim-witted. If I did eventually join a congregation in, say, middle age, when I had nothing better to occupy my time, it would be as a nominal member of the Episcopal Church. (I perceived the Episcopalians as the country club set—small-town royalty—and thus people of precisely the caliber I hoped to become.)

Not much has turned out as I expected. My prelaw classes at the University of Kentucky taught me almost nothing except that the reading of law, while no doubt edifying to other young men and women, bored me comatose. The law was for me a kind of academic sensory deprivation.

And after wallowing for several years in a bacchanalia of, literally and intentionally, godless hedonism, I found that I missed the caring Maker about whom I'd heard so often as a boy in Sunday school. The harder I partied, the emptier I felt.

Reluctantly, even ashamedly, I finally gave up my dream of practicing law and, simultaneously, returned to my low-church origins, in both cases because I didn't want to shoot myself from despair.

In the twenty years that since have passed, I've evolved into, variously, a college graduate (three times), a journalist, an author, and now the full-time copastor (with my father, he whose clerical calling had left me stone cold as a youth) of a rural church near the foothills of eastern Kentucky's rugged Appalachian Mountains.

As I said, I don't know for sure what all these evolutions and revolutions mean, how I ended up being who I apparently have become. Some days I'm not certain what anything means. But I began publicly telling some of my life's stories and pondering my questions almost a decade ago, after the editors of the *Lexington Herald-Leader*, the newspaper where I then worked, took leave of their senses and made me the paper's religion reporter.

Among the duties assigned me by my immediate supervisor, Paula Anderson, was the writing of a weekly column about faith. Initially I balked. The idea of writing an opinion column certainly appealed to my ego. But I knew religion to be an exceedingly dangerous topic. Kentucky sometimes is described as the buckle on the Bible Belt. A great many people here take their churchgoing almost as seriously as they take the University of Kentucky basketball program. Question either institution and you're liable to receive heartfelt invitations to an old-fashioned necktie party right out of *The Ox-Bow Incident*, a soiree in which you're intended to be guest of honor.

However, after some urging by Paula, I nervously blundered ahead—and received one of the great surprises of my life. For the first time in my lackluster newspaper career, I started receiving fan mail. I don't mean a letter or two, either. I got so many letters I couldn't answer them all, so many that periodically I'd drag them from the newsroom to my car in one of those huge Hefty garbage bags.

Of course I heard from the necktie-party crowd, too. But mostly the letters were positive, even gushy. They came from across the religious and irreligious spectrum: Baptists, Buddhists, Presbyterians, Pentecostals, Catholics, Jews, and, oddly, atheists. I heard from priests, university presidents, and prisoners in our state's penal institutions.

I learned that I'd stumbled onto what I can only suppose must be a widely felt longing in the late twentieth century, a desire to regain some lost sense of the transcendent. As I continued to write about my bittersweet memories of country revival meetings, or my mixed feelings about my devout family members, or my ongoing struggles to trust a God Who declines to show Himself directly—or, on occasion, about my little spiritual victories and insights—people wrote me back long and moving letters about their own memories, beliefs, fears, and triumphs.

One complex theme pervaded many of the responses. Men and women said they hoped to learn about God, yet often they seemed unable or unwilling to look for their answers in churches or synagogues. Many felt they'd been burned earlier by organized religion.

Slowly during my time at the *Herald-Leader*, and later as I made the transition into the pastoral ministry, I increasingly perceived a need for a book such as this, which would try to address some of those common spiritual desires and dilemmas that all of us, churchgoers or not, face—but in a contemplative, comfortable, and nonaggressive tone.

Eventually I selected a format based upon the traditional Judeo-Christian habit of worshiping weekly: fifty-two short, nonsectarian essays, one for each week of the year. Each piece is followed by a meditation, a prayer of sorts that we can recall when the world inevitably starts again to clang and wail around us.

Read these pieces whenever you wish, of course, but I like the biblical notion that we should set aside a day each week especially to seek our Maker. That ancient law often has been abused, but originally it was intended to assure us all of a regularly scheduled time for quietly cleansing our minds and remembering that we are mortal, a day for laying aside the buzz of the marketplace and seeking the comfort of our loved ones.

I've chosen not to follow the liturgical calendar, a decision sure to irritate a few readers. My experience is that faith, or the search for it, doesn't necessarily follow a liturgical pattern. And for good or ill, this book is based largely on my own experiences in my quest to get to know the Unknowable One. I did pay homage in their appropriate seasons to the annual rituals and holidays familiar to most Americans, including Passover, Easter, summer softball, Halloween, Thanksgiving, and Christmas. But mainly I allowed the fifty-two pieces to lie where they fell.

In any case, I wrote these essays to encourage you—and me—to contemplate the spiritual issues we should (whatever day each of us might set apart): our Creator's grace, the fleetingness of time, the fulfillment or loss of our youthful dreams, our need to appreciate and be appreciated by our kin. These are matters we can ponder whether we happen to be sitting in a Sunday-school class or enjoying a weekend camping trip in the mountains. Good luck and Godspeed to you in your journey.

PAUL PRATHER
Mount Sterling, Kentucky

BACK PORCH
❖ FAITH ❖

THE WORLD OPERATES ON SPIRITUAL LAWS, TOO

I once interviewed country singer Naomi Judd, who with her daughter Wynonna made up the acclaimed duet The Judds.

Naomi had been forced to give up her singing career. A former nurse, she had contracted a chronic and potentially deadly strain of hepatitis, probably from a needle stick. She and Wynonna had finished an emotional good-bye tour, and Naomi mostly was confined to her Tennessee farm, battling for her life.

I spoke with her over the phone. She told me matter-of-factly that she expected to recover from her incurable disease.

Science offered her little hope, she said, but she'd been walking in the woods on her farm, singing Gregorian chants. She'd renewed her faith in God. She'd begun consulting experts from several academic and religious disciplines who believed in the mind's power to heal the body and in God's power to heal the mind.

"I've learned that this world operates as much on spiritual laws as on scientific ones," she said.

I've long since lost touch with Judd, but as I write this I've recently seen news accounts about her on national television.

Doctors have declared her totally free of the incurable hepatitis that once wracked her body and wrecked her career.

And I've been thinking again of what she told me: *This world operates as much on spiritual laws as on scientific ones.*

We forget sometimes, living in the technological culture of the West, that our rationalistic approach to problems is the minority worldview. On most of our planet, the vast majority of humans continue to think just as their, and our, ancestors did for millennia, that the realm of the spiritual is every bit as potent as the realm of the physical.

Worldwide, Pentecostal Christians continue to prophesy and speak in tongues, believing that the God of the Bible talks through them just as God spoke through the first-century apostles. In China, government leaders seek out Buddhist chi gong healers to cure their illnesses by passing hands over the afflicted portions of their bodies. In Africa, villagers see spirits who take on the forms of leopards and monkeys.

We westerners reflexively tend to assume that such people just aren't as smart as we are. That's arrogant of us. As a rationalistic scholar once admitted to me, there simply are too many accounts of supernatural phenomena to ignore them all; it's unlikely that hundreds of millions of humans could be utterly deluded over thousands of years.

He was right, of course.

Increasingly, for me the eeriest evidence in favor of life's spiritual dimension lies within science itself.

For instance, the Big Bang theory of the universe's origins

argues that billions of years ago the entire universe existed in a lifeless, unimaginably dense core. For some reason this core exploded and hurled out from itself at incredible velocity the first elements of matter that would, over eons, develop into the stars, planets, and people we see today. It's still exploding.

But a few scientists also have acknowledged a problem with calling this event the "Big Bang." You see, when the universe's core exploded, oxygen didn't yet exist. Without oxygen, there would have been nothing to conduct the explosion's sound.

Thus, there was no "bang"—there was, instead, only a massive eruption of light.

Scientists prefer the term "Big Bang," one of them has written, because the more accurate description, "Big Light," is a tad too theological. "Big Light" bears too close a resemblance to the Bible's description of the universe's birth.

Genesis tells us that the cosmos began like this: "God said, 'Let there be light'; and there was light." An obvious question is how the writer of Genesis, living in a primitive, prescientific desert culture, could have anticipated by three millennia the most profound theory of cosmology developed by modern physicists and astronomers.

The Bible itself explains such mysteries by claiming that God revealed Earth's origins to Moses.

Through the centuries, religious seers from a variety of traditions have managed to predict, with what Israeli physicist Gerald L. Schroeder calls "unnerving" accuracy, recent cosmological breakthroughs, using the ancient Scriptures as their guide.

In the 1200s the great Jewish thinker Nahmanides wrote that in the briefest moments following creation, the entire universe existed in a compressed form so tiny it was about the size of a grain of mustard seed. From this microscopic substance came everything that has been, is, or ever will be in the physical universe.

Proponents of the Big Bang theory, such as Schroeder, now agree that the entire universe started as an incredibly dense point no bigger than a mote of dust. As Schroeder describes it in his book *Genesis and the Big Bang*, at its beginning the universe could barely have been viewed through a microscope. Everything that exists came from a speck of dust, a grain of mustard seed.

There are many such inexplicable examples. An astronomer named Hugh Ross says the ancient biblical scribes described up to ten dimensions of time and space, well beyond the four dimensions with which humans then were familiar. Physicists in our century have demonstrated that such multiple dimensions do exist.

The longer I live, the more I believe we should not assume the world is a purely mechanistic place. There also is, all around us, a hidden kingdom of the spirit. The cosmos indeed operates on spiritual laws as well as on physical ones. Only faith can open our eyes to see these truths and comprehend these laws.

THIS WEEK'S MEDITATION:

"God of creation, I want to see beyond the limits of my physical eyes. Show me the spiritual truths taught by faith. Forgive me for the times I've been arrogant, when I've assumed my view of the world is the only legitimate one."

2 **Week**

TIME'S HEADLIGHTS

I was a week or so from my thirty-fifth birthday. Suddenly Time came hurtling at me like a runaway '56 Cadillac careening down a Kentucky mountain in the night, its horn screaming. I found myself staring at the grillwork of middle age and what would follow that, paralyzed in the headlights. Like anybody who sees his death's approach, I started thinking back that day. It seemed to me the truths I'd come to know weren't at all what I'd expected to know when I turned thirty-five.

A lot is written about abused children and their subsequent problems. Rightly so. But nobody ever mentions the pain that can result from having been treated too well.

For six years, until the birth of my sister, I was the only child of two dedicated parents. Even after my sister's birth, I was doted upon. My mom and dad had grown up poor. They wanted more for me. They loved me beyond the bounds of good sense.

"You're special," my mom told me. "You're smart."

"Anything anyone else can do, you can do better," my dad said.

My parents had the best intentions, but as a kid I responded wrongly, by thinking I was the center of all existence. I learned early that you can travel far on mere ego if you have more of it than those around you. People less certain of themselves tend to believe your self-assurance.

In high school I was voted president of my class, most popular in my class, a member of the student council. I was a varsity football player. My dad, who could barely meet our monthly bills, hocked his soul to buy me a flashy sports car. I dated a majorette.

I also became an unbearable snob, condescending toward people who weren't as lucky as I was. I made jokes about ugly girls. I bedeviled awkward guys. I had too many hormones and too few brains. I figured I'd rule high school, zip through college, go to law school. I'd somehow be worth a half million bucks by the time I was twenty-five, and a millionaire at thirty.

Then it was all gone.

Initially it had looked as if I might become an all-state football player before I graduated from high school. But between my junior and senior seasons my football coach left to take a college job. He was replaced by a coach who didn't like my attitude. Instead of collecting trophies, I spent my last season collecting splinters on the bench.

After graduation, I didn't set off for a large university with my buddies. I attended a nearby Baptist college because I wanted to be close to my sweetheart, who had a year of high school left. Early in my freshman year my girlfriend and I broke up, and I was stranded at this conservative school with no love and a busted heart. So I went into a funky, longhaired, rebel-without-a-clue stage. I didn't fit in then with students who were studying to be preachers. I began hanging out with the school's few outcasts.

Soon I transferred to the University of Kentucky, where I became a microscopic fish in an infinite sea of handsome, wealthy, blond kids.

I dropped out of college altogether and into the worst recession since the 1930s. For the next few years I worked as a janitor, a building painter, a substitute schoolteacher, a newspaper carrier. I never made more than $6,000 in a year.

As I entered adulthood, I gained weight. My eyes went bad. I had to wear glasses. Here I was, the same guy who had laughed at the fat and the nearsighted.

At about the time in life that I'd expected to be a rich young legal whiz, I found myself clerking in a department store for minimum wage. By then, I'd had a long time to realize I was less intelligent than I'd believed, weaker, less self-sufficient. Formerly it had appeared to me that people who weren't as fortunate as I somehow didn't have the same loves, the same goals, the same hurts. I asked God to forgive me for the pain I'd caused.

And my life gradually turned again. I married a woman who loved me. She helped me go back to college, this time with my priorities straight. I studied hard. We had a fine son. Eventually I landed a job writing for a good newspaper, making a tolerable living at what I liked best. I won a few prizes.

But that melancholy day as my thirty-fifth birthday pressed upon me, I pondered where I'd come from, and where to that point I'd ended up. I realized I'd failed at most of the things I'd hoped to accomplish.

That same night, my wife and son and I sat in our living room playing a card game. I lost. We laughed.

After Renee put our boy to bed, I turned on the stereo, the volume low. Merle Haggard's sad, raspy voice wafted through our tiny apartment, a song about a man who has spent his life searching for the lucky break that will bring him wealth and self-worth. His dreams never have been fulfilled, but still his wife has remained alongside him.

Wearing sweat suits and old slippers, Renee and I slow-danced. As we shuffled across the carpet, I experienced one of those rare moments of clarity we mortals occasionally are granted. I realized that, almost without noticing how, I'd actually attained everything for which I reasonably could ask in this world, more than the majority of the planet's inhabitants ever get: a warm place to live, a healthy child, a kind wife. It had taken me ten hard years to pull my life around that far.

I'd visited the heights of my small-town world, and then I'd smacked my chin on the bottom, and suddenly that night I found myself more than happy with what I'd regained, meager as it might have seemed to some.

I saw also how precarious that happiness was for me—for all of us. No matter who we think we are, our lives and our lifestyles are but vapors. A wrong word, a disease, a change in bosses, and we are laid waste in an instant. That knowledge, of life's brittleness, should make sweeter those brief moments when we do find joy.

Here's what I decided that evening: We're all standing together on that mountain highway, with Time's headlights coming on, on. There's nowhere to go.

What can we do?

We can cower. We can writhe with bitterness at our unfulfilled dreams. Or, in the few moments we have, in the headlights' glaring beams, we can wrap our arms around someone we love. And dance.

THIS WEEK'S MEDITATION:

*"My losses and victories alike are bound to vanish soon.
Until then, let me recognize those who love me.
Let me support them when they would falter, and let me be humble
enough to lean against them when my own knees sag."*

IT'S NEVER TOO LATE
TO FORGIVE

My wife, Renee, has a distant relative named Dean Martin, like the old TV star. He's a friend of mine, a doting father and a devout Christian. Dean hails from a legalistic religious tradition, though. He learned early to take the Bible literally—and to dismiss people who didn't see things his way.

Some years ago Renee's brother, Gordon, decided to get married. His bride, Sheila, had been married before and divorced. That was a real problem for Dean. In the Bible, Jesus says that anyone who divorces and then marries again is committing adultery, because in God's sight when you marry for the first time, you're wed forever. Only by death do you part.

This marriage, then, bothered Dean. So he refused to come to the wedding, even though he was kin. He wasn't really rude, but he didn't hide his reasons. Plainly, he didn't intend to be a party to sin.

Time does interesting things to us all. Eventually, Gordon and Sheila and Dean all ended up attending the same country church where I then was the part-time pastor. As far as I know, no one ever brought up Gordon and Sheila's wedding or Dean's actions.

11

Meanwhile, Dean's oldest son grew up and got married. Then he divorced. Then he married again.

I was present at the son's second wedding. So was Dean, not that I was surprised. I knew love wouldn't let him miss his own son's ceremony.

The next day, Dean, Gordon, Sheila, and I ended up congregated in our church's vestibule after the Sunday morning service. Dean, standing between Gordon and Sheila, suddenly reached out and embraced the couple warmly.

"I want you two to forgive me," he said, loudly enough for anyone in that end of the church to hear.

Gordon and Sheila appeared a little confused.

"Forgive you for what?" my brother-in-law said.

"Years ago, when you got married, I wouldn't come to your wedding," Dean said. "I was doing what I thought was right. But God's given me light on that subject I didn't have then. I'm sorry. I wish you'd forgive me."

Gordon and Sheila smiled.

"We forgive you," Gordon said.

"We never held it against you to begin with," Sheila said.

And that pretty much was that. Except that everyone appeared to feel a lot better, even though a minute earlier I hadn't realized anyone was feeling bad. Even I felt better, and none of it had anything to do with me.

Afterward, I mulled over what I'd witnessed. I talked with Dean.

It occurred to me that life has a way of smacking all of us in the face with our own smug actions. What we condemn in others invariably returns as a flaw in our own lives or in our immediate families. It's as if God is heaven-bent on reminding us that we're not perfect enough to judge people.

I posed this idea to Dean, who agreed. But he told me that his apology wasn't based so much on his son's situation. He said it was more that anyone who is serious about his faith—and he is—tends to grow spiritually over time, to learn new lessons, to soften.

Still, I marveled at the potential for healing that resides in genuine sorrow and in genuine forgiveness. Dean had found it in his heart to forgive Gordon and Sheila for what he took to be their transgression. He asked for, and got, their forgiveness for his own wrong.

Many of us regret certain things we've done, whether or not we can summon the courage to publicly apologize. We all hope to be forgiven by God and our neighbors.

But no religious mandate is more difficult than the reciprocal one, which demands that to receive the forgiveness we crave, we must first forgive those who have wronged us.

In *Christianity Today* magazine, writer Philip Yancey once explored this daunting law, using as tests such news events as "ethnic cleansing" by Serbs.

Yancey asked, "Is forgiveness logical?"

No, he decided. It's unforgiveness, not forgiveness, that has at its core a "terrible, crystalline logic": an eye for an eye, a tooth for a tooth.

He asked, "Is forgiveness just?"

No again. "In a world of unspeakable atrocity," Yancey wrote, "forgiveness seems unjust, unfair. . . . As the philosopher Herbert Marcuse put it, 'One cannot, and should not, go around happily killing and torturing and then, when the moment has come, simply ask, and receive, forgiveness.'"

But should we—as individuals and as societies—forgive each other anyway?

Yes, Yancey said. Serbian ethnic cleansing, for instance, is the result of centuries of feuding, demands for justice, and repeated reprisals by various groups in the Balkans.

"What happened to Yugoslavia illustrates the one thing that unfair, irrational forgiveness has going for it: It is the alternative," Yancey said. "Where unforgiveness reigns, as essayist Lance Morrow has pointed out, a Newtonian law comes into play: For every atrocity, there must be an equal and opposite atrocity."

Or, as Gandhi said, if everyone were to follow the principle of an eye for an eye, soon the whole world would go blind.

The commandment of forgiveness, then, might not be easy, fair, or logical, but it both frees the person who is forgiven and saves the forgiver's life and soul.

I admit that it's a complicated and difficult undertaking, trying to get over the wrongs we've committed and the wrongs we've suffered.

Still, I wonder how many rifts in this world might be mended if someone would just say, unbidden: "I'm sorry." And if the injured person could respond: "I forgive you. I forgave you before you asked."

THIS WEEK'S MEDITATION:

"God, I've wronged others, and I feel guilty about it. I've been wronged, too, and I feel even worse about that. Some days I'm vengeful. Other days I want to be set free from this burden of anger. Give me the courage to tell those I've hurt that I'm sorry. Then, in Your power, let me start the process of forgiving those who have hurt me. Let me be the one who ends the cycle of wrath."

4 **Week**

THE POWER OF PRAYER IS A COMFORT

Normally I'm not a fan of bumper stickers, but one I've seen happens to be truer than most. It says, "Prayer changes things."

Evidently prayer does help. Certainly it's awfully popular for some reason.

Here are a few bits of information about prayer, from *Newsweek* magazine:

- Both prayer and secular meditation measurably reduce the medical symptoms of stress. But prayer to God or Jesus is more effective than is a secular mantra.

- Ninety-one percent of women pray; 85 percent of men do.

- Ten percent of those who don't believe in God still pray daily.

- Prayer is a favorite topic among readers. There are two thousand books on prayer and meditation, three times the number on sex.

- Actually, prayer and sex might be related. Surveys by Roman Catholic sociologist Andrew Greeley show that combining frequent sex with frequent prayer makes for the most satisfying marriages.

- Those who report feeling "led by God" during prayer are more likely to be forgiving, politically active, and satisfied with their lives than are other folks.

If your parents taught you to kneel by your bedside each evening and offer up a word of thanks or a request for divine guidance, they probably were doing you a favor. If they didn't teach you to pray, it's never too late to pick up the habit.

Still, for many of us, even those of us who grew up attending church or temple, prayer doesn't always happen easily. For one thing, unless we're faced with an immediate crisis such as the nosedive of the jet on which we're riding (or at least a painful trip to the dentist), prayer usually requires self-discipline; there's so much competition for our time. For another thing, trying to talk with the Almighty can be intimidating. And let's face it, the silence on the other end of the line often tends to be deafening.

I think that's why Jesus' earliest disciples once went to Him and asked, "Lord, teach us to pray." Probably they weren't getting the results they desired from their prayers, any more than we do.

When Jesus prayed, storms fell silent and fish multiplied and the dead came walking out of their tombs still wrapped in

17

their grave clothes. What the disciples really meant was, "Tell us how you *do* that."

In answer, Jesus gave them what's now called the Model Prayer or, more popularly, the Lord's Prayer.

I've considered it for a long time. I haven't begun to mine all its secrets, but I have uncovered one small gem: When I interject myself into Jesus' prayer, it seems to bring me more peace than I receive from merely reciting the biblical words. I pray it like this:

Our Father which art in heaven, hallowed be Thy name . . .

"I like to call you 'our precious heavenly Father' because that makes me think of my dad's dad, Fred Prather. He began all his prayers that way. Thinking of him makes me think, too, of my mother's father, Oscar Chestnut, and of my own dad. Those three earthly fathers nurtured me with their love, concern, and power.

"Because You are my heavenly Father, I believe You are even more loving and concerned and powerful than they were.

"And unlike my earthly fathers, You are flawless. Their intentions were good, but their means occasionally were wrong. Yours never are wrong. You're always right. You're always just. You're always good. Thank you."

Thy kingdom come . . .

"Jesus said the kingdom of God is in our hearts. Let me recognize that kingdom in myself and in others. Help me act according to its two central laws: Love God and love your neighbor as yourself."

Thy will be done in earth, as it is in heaven . . .

"I've heard that in heaven there's no pain, there's no sickness, there's no heartbreak, there's no poverty. Make the earth a little more like that. Help me to help You make the world a little more like that."

Give us this day our daily bread . . .

"Give me today what I need for today: money, health, and patience enough to survive. Help me believe You'll do the same tomorrow. I want to accept the past for what it was, because I can't change a moment of it. I want to quit worrying about the future, because I don't know whether it will be good or bad, and I can't control it anyway. I want to learn to live in this present moment, because it's the only moment I really have."

And forgive us our debts, as we forgive our debtors . . .

"I'm sorry, but I'm a knothead a good deal of the time. Forgive me, just as I'm trying my best to forgive the knotheads with whom I must deal."

And lead us not into temptation, but deliver us from evil . . .

"There are a lot of destructive sins in this world, and I'm tempted to commit most of them. That just seems to be my nature. But You can cause those temptations to pass me by without calling my name.

"Please do that. Please protect me from myself. Don't let me do anything stupid that would hurt me or those I love or, for that matter, those I don't particularly love."

For Thine is the kingdom, and the power, and the glory, forever. Amen.

"When all is said and done, Lord, everything belongs to You. It began with You, and it will end with You. You're God, and I'm not, and I'm darned glad on both counts.

"So be it."

THIS WEEK'S MEDITATION:

"Lord, teach me to pray in a manner that brings results."

WHEN GOD SEEMS
CAPRICIOUS

I became serious about my faith in God twenty years ago through the intervention of a wonderful little congregation of Christians that took me under its collective wing. I was a rowdy young man, and reforming me became kind of a group project.

By some folks' standards, the people in this church were quirky. For instance, they believed God was still working supernaturally through divine healing and prophecy.

But I liked what I saw in them. They genuinely loved their enemies, of whom, given their unusual beliefs, they had gained more than a few. They were full of vibrant joy. When they told me God still routinely performed miracles, I said, "Okay."

And I did see some things that I'm certain were acts of God. I even experienced a few such acts myself, to my own astonishment.

At the time, I was single and living with my parents and my teenage sister, Cathi. One day, Cathi slipped and fell. She walked into the house in tears, holding an arm that obviously was broken. An awkward indentation pocked the middle of her forearm, where bones were supposed to be.

"We need to get you to the emergency room," my dad said, turning pale.

My sister—who wasn't terribly religious—suddenly said, "Would you all pray?"

I placed the fingertips of my right hand as lightly as possible over the broken spot. Cathi, my dad, and I quickly bowed our heads and shut our eyes. I mumbled an impromptu and not particularly confident prayer.

As I prayed, the bones in Cathi's arm moved beneath my fingers. Dumbfounded, I opened my eyes to find Cathi staring at me, her eyes equally wide.

"Did you feel that?" she said.

Instantly, her arm had set itself . . . or had been set, I should say. The indentation was gone. No emergency room. No cast. The "broken" arm developed a slight bruise and a little puffiness, but nothing else. Within forty-eight hours, it was normal.

Months later, one of the people I admired most in the little church I attended, a middle-aged woman named Wilma, was diagnosed with cancer. She didn't seem particularly distressed by her disease. She had the simple faith that God would heal her. We prayed for her. We continued praying for months.

She wasted away and died.

That's when I came face to face with this tension inherent in religion, a tension that predates even Christianity. Namely, most faiths claim their god is loving, at least toward the faithful. They also claim their god is all-powerful. And yet daily people get sick

22

and die. They get mangled in car crashes. Innocent babies are born with AIDS.

In short, occasionally God acts in spectacular, sea-parting, water-walking ways. But mostly He doesn't. People in trouble continue to suffer: good people and bad, the faithful and the faithless.

So there's a basic contradiction in our beliefs. That is, if God does indeed love us and yet doesn't prevent our suffering, then He appears not to possess much power. If, on the other hand, God is all-powerful and allows us to suffer anyway, then either He must not be very caring or He at least plays favorites, choosing to bless one and ignore another.

Philosophers and theologians have wrestled with this dilemma for centuries. The ancient Platonists finally reconciled the problem by deciding their gods weren't really very mighty. The Epicureans said the gods were strong, but just didn't give a fig one way or the other what happened to mere mortals. The Stoics, interestingly, declared that suffering wasn't really suffering; it was only an errant state of mind.

Christianity always has tried to hold the contradictions in some sort of equilibrium. God is love, it says. God is all-powerful. But people often suffer because God also allows evil to exist.

Why does God do that? Some Christians tell me that enduring pain helps strengthen and mature us. Others say we suffer because of our sins—that we've misused the free will God gave us. None of the theories, from the Epicurean to the Christian, fully satisfies me. I've never been able to sort it out.

I put a lot of stock in the Judeo-Christian Scriptures. If the Bible tells us anything, it's that God is a personal God. From Genesis, where God walks with Adam and Eve, to Revelation, where Jesus reveals Himself to John in a vision, one principle is clear: God cares about individuals and touches their lives in matters great and small.

Yet He allows people to suffer. Jesus is crucified. Stephen gets martyred.

Sometimes even today the apparent contradictions in God's actions seem absurd. Why would God heal my sister's broken arm and not heal my friend's cancer?

I don't know.

That, I think, is where faith, mystery, and reverence become important. Staring at such conundrums, we're faced with crucial choices. We can dismiss God as a vindictive fraud—or we can admit that God's ways might be higher than ours, that perhaps we aren't capable of apprehending His plans. We can decide that we understand more about right and wrong than God does and constantly second-guess Him, or we can trust that God knows more than we do and bow to Him.

I choose to bow. I believe in God, but I often don't have a clue what He's doing.

THIS WEEK'S MEDITATION:

*"God, one thing I don't like about faith
is that it's not always logical, at least as I define logic.
There are times when I'm not sure I even like You, because You do
things I find unpleasant. Despite all this, I continue to believe.
How about giving me some help today with my faith?"*

6 **Week**

MORE ON SPIRITUAL LAWS

We understand that certain natural laws govern our physical world. For instance, there's the law of gravity. Gravity generally is a good thing. It keeps us from being tossed off our rotating planet into outer space. But if we ignore it, gravity can kill us.

I remember an accident I read about in a newspaper many years ago. Several college students who happened to be staying in a hotel took the psychedelic drug LSD. One girl, hallucinating, decided that gravity didn't apply to her anymore. She believed she could fly. She threw herself from the balcony of the hotel room, expecting to soar into the sky. Instead, she crashed to the sidewalk several stories below and died. She didn't believe in gravity, but that didn't make it any less real. The law of gravity worked whether or not she happened to accept it.

As I mentioned earlier in this book, just as physical laws govern our lives, certain spiritual laws control us as well. These spiritual laws are as real as the physical ones. We can choose to accept them or deny them, but in either case they'll exercise their power. They affect everyone, religious or not. They're built into the fabric of the universe.

This observation isn't original with me. Among the clearest

explanations of spiritual laws I've read is a 1982 book by TV minister Pat Robertson, *The Secret Kingdom*. I don't follow Robertson's guidance on every issue. I've been bothered at times by his politics and some of his financial dealings. Still, you don't have to agree with a person on every matter to recognize when he's gotten something correct. And when Robertson talks about God's universal spiritual rules, I agree with him 100 percent. He didn't discover these rules, either; they're familiar to any moderately serious student of the New Testament. But Robertson named and categorized them in an easy-to-grasp way.

Here are a few of the laws he identifies:

The Law of Reciprocity. This law says that what you give in this world is pretty much what you'll receive in return. If you smile at a stranger, he'll likely smile back. If you snarl at him, he'll snarl at you. In Luke 6, Jesus says, "As you would have people do to you, do exactly the same to them." This principle doesn't just affect our dealings with other people. It's also a key to our dealings with God Himself. Jesus said that if we forgive others, God will forgive us; if we don't, He won't.

The Law of Use. In every arena—education, farming, finances, faith, weight lifting—what you consistently use multiplies. And what you don't use, you lose. This law is plainly taught in the parable of the talents, found in Matthew 25.

Finding contemporary illustrations for it is no problem. If you study the French language in college for four or five semesters and then spend a few weeks living in Paris, you'll be amazed at how fluent you've become. Stop taking French classes and speaking the language, and within a year or two you'll have forgotten everything you knew.

Or let's say you save up $100. If you blow it on a night on the town, you'll have nothing. But what if you invest that same $100 and by hard work manage to double it each year? After one year, you'll have $200. After five long years, it will have grown to just $3,200. Keep at that pace for ten years and you'll be worth $102,400. Continue for thirty years and your $100 will have exploded into $107 billion.

The Law of Perseverance. Your middle-school coach was right: Quitters never win, and winners never quit. To succeed at anything, you must be endlessly persistent. This is true even of prayer. In Matthew 7, to cite one example, Jesus says—in the earliest Greek words—that God gives to those who "keep on asking." The door of spiritual revelation is opened to those who "keep on seeking."

The Law of Greatness. There are many paradoxes in the spiritual world. One is this: Jesus explained that the person who would become the mightiest must first be eager to serve others. Armies have recognized this for centuries. The most effective officers are those who tend to their soldiers' needs for food and shelter before looking to their own needs. They lead from the front. Their soldiers, inspired by their example, will follow them through the gates of hell if necessary.

The Law of Unity. A house divided against itself can't stand, the Scriptures say. Conversely, a house united is nearly impossible to bring down.

We've all seen this. A husband and wife who love and emotionally support each other can weather any problem: unemployment, sickness, unruly children. A couple working against each other can destroy their entire family, for several generations. Backbiting, jealousy, and grumbling are deadly. They undermine unity.

Unity doesn't double our strength; unity multiplies it. If one mighty warrior can put to flight one thousand of the enemy, the Bible says, two fighting together can overwhelm ten thousand. That's why Jesus always sent out his disciples in pairs. When two of them locked arms in a common faith, their unity brought God's power into their midst.

There are other laws as well, some of which we'll examine in later weeks. If you learn to recognize and master a few of these principles you'll rapidly see the quality of your life change for the better.

THIS WEEK'S MEDITATION:

"Creator of the universe, allow me to understand the spiritual laws that govern the cosmos just as a scientist understands the laws of physics or biology. Then give me the wisdom and self-discipline to master these spiritual rules, rather than being mastered by them."

THE LAW OF SOWING AND REAPING

Here's another spiritual law that explains much of what happens around us, whether we're talking about the beans in our vegetable gardens, the dynamics of our individual families, or political tensions among the nations.

It's been called the law of sowing and reaping. Saint Paul explains it succinctly in the biblical book of Galatians: "Don't be deceived; you can't mock God. For whatever you sow, that will you also reap."

The principle of sowing and reaping is present throughout the Scriptures. In Genesis, God announces that as long as the earth exists, the cycle of seedtime and harvest will never end. It soon becomes clear He's talking about more than farming. In the Gospels, Jesus tells several parables about the sowing of seeds—and claims these stories explain how God's whole kingdom functions.

Everything, it seems, begins as a kind of "seed." Major corporations start with an idea in some entrepreneur's mind that, with much tending, grows into a mom-and-pop business, which grows into a conglomerate. Every tribe begins with the fertilizing of a seed between one man and one woman. Gradually, that seed

31

grows into a baby, who grows into an adult, who joins with an-other person and sows more seeds; the family continually mul-tiplies until nations can result.

A friend from my boyhood once approached me with a business offer. He'd become heavily involved in marketing a cer-tain business service. He believed in this service so strongly that he'd quit his job as a schoolteacher and had gone on the road as a commission-only salesman, with no guarantee of an income. Driven by the potential he saw, he was working night and day. He was "sowing" to this company with all his might.

He asked whether I wanted to join him. No thanks, I said. I had a secure job making a decent salary. I didn't like selling. I wasn't sure his venture would work out.

Gradually, as he grew ever busier and busier, I lost touch with my friend. But a couple of years later I read a magazine ar-ticle about him and what a success his venture had become. It said he personally was earning $12 million a year in commis-sions.

I'm not earning $12 million a year. At the rate I'm going I won't earn half that much altogether in my whole life. Am I jealous of my pal? No. He's just reaping the results of having sown to his business faithfully, over a long period of time, at great personal hardship and risk. I'm reaping the results—or lack of results—of not having tended my garden alongside his, of not having shared his vision.

The principle of sowing and reaping tells us, at least in part, why some marriages succeed and others fail, why certain churches gain influence and others wither, why some people experience an intimate relationship with God and others never hear from Him.

It's because this law works for you or against you, but it always works. It works for the godly and the ungodly; it's no respecter of persons. Everyone reaps pretty much what he or she sows. If you plant an orange tree, it won't sprout apples. If you sow only potatoes in your garden, you won't harvest corn.

Do you want to raise happy, responsible children? Then focus more effort on them than you give to your job or your favorite basketball team or the country club. Read all the books you can find on child rearing. Arrange your schedule to spend as much time as possible with your kids. Attend their school events. Shower them with love. Discipline them consistently. Teach them high morals. Treat their mother or father with respect.

If you sow faithfully to your job as a parent, the chances are overwhelming that your children will make you proud. If you don't do these things, don't be shocked when your kids turn out to be dunderheads.

Sure, I know, there are exceptions. Particularly when we're dealing with human "seeds," as in trying to raise children or make marriages work, we must recognize that there are other people involved who possess free wills. They also choose to sow seeds. You might devote your whole life to your husband, but if he just flat refuses to be happy and faithful, your marriage could fail anyway. It happens that way sometimes. But those unhappy cases are the exception, not the rule. Nearly always you reap what you sow.

There's one additional point here. If you expect to reap a bountiful reward in any area of life, you must keep sowing your seeds and weeding your garden until the harvest arrives. That can take quite a while. You might grow tomato plants in a few weeks, but redwood trees—and children—take years to reach maturity.

If you quit too soon, or if you sow inconsistently, you'll never get your reward. You've got to keep tending your crops until the harvest comes.

Most people just aren't willing to do that. You can be the exception.

THIS WEEK'S MEDITATION:

"Lord, help me choose my seeds wisely, sow them consistently, and tend them diligently. Let me understand that every day I am creating my own future—and others' futures as well."

DESIRE MAKES A DIFFERENCE

Dan Jenkins's comic sports novel *Semi-Tough* features among its memorable characters a New York Giants football player named Shake Tiller.

In one scene Shake and his teammate Billy Clyde Puckett are discussing an all-pro defensive back who plays for their cross-town rivals, the New York Jets, which the Giants are soon to face in the Super Bowl. The two Giants fear this other guy, Dreamer Tatum, because he always pulls off one spectacular play after another, game after game.

Billy Clyde asks Shake how Dreamer manages to keep doing that.

"Wants to," Shake says simply.

The book is fiction, but the statement is truth. It's amazing how much difference "want-to" can make.

In 1993 a native of my home state won the Nobel Prize in medicine. Phillip Sharp was at the time a biology professor at the Massachusetts Institute of Technology.

It's not every year that a fellow Kentuckian wins a Nobel Prize, so I took a special interest in reading about Sharp. As it turned out, he hadn't grown up as the scion of an aristocratic family in our state's old-money Bluegrass region. He'd grown up instead on a small farm. He hadn't graduated from Lexington's exclusive Sayre School, but from Pendleton County High School, a modest alma mater even by the anemic standards of Kentucky's public education system. Sharp then had raised calves to pay his tuition at tiny Union College in Barbourville, Kentucky.

"He didn't have a lot of the opportunities kids have now," his former high school biology teacher told one newspaper. "We had one biology room and a little lab not much bigger than a closet. He's done this all on his own."

That's precisely the point I've longed for someone to make about education—and about life. It's not so much the quality of an institution's faculty that makes the difference in a student's ability to learn and succeed. It's not the size of a school's computer lab or its willingness to seek out minorities or to bankroll the economically disadvantaged. Surely all those things are important, and I'm in favor of improving them.

Still, as Sharp's Nobel Prize reminded me, the central component of educational and professional betterment is a personal one. It's want-to. Guts. Drive. Doggedness. Character.

In addition, it doesn't hurt if you're gifted with a parent or preacher or teacher who drills into you a sense of your abilities and responsibilities. But even then the burden finally falls on you.

My dad was raised as the youngest of five children in an impoverished southeastern Kentucky household. The series of houses in which his family lived mostly lacked indoor plumbing and central heat. Nonetheless, Dad graduated from high school, itself a feat. Then he graduated from college, too, the first in our large family to do so.

He attended college by working a semester to save money for tuition and then enrolling in classes the next semester, and then sitting out the next semester to work again. He earned a master's degree as well.

He wanted to.

Later, I graduated from high school in Kentucky's old Fifth Congressional District, then the most poorly educated district in America. Like Sharp's school, mine had no computers. We didn't even have an electric typewriter, to my knowledge. When one of our classrooms got a new globe it was a big deal.

Certainly many of my schoolmates received hardly any education at all there; they dropped out of school at sixteen and ended up in prison, on dope, or on welfare. I never knew anyone who won a Nobel Prize or is likely to. But I did know people who attended the same school and nevertheless persevered through twelfth grade and then college and then continued on to laudable professional accomplishments. At least one earned a degree from Harvard; another attended the U.S. Naval Academy. Others became geologists, entrepreneurs, or teachers.

They wanted to.

I knew a black kid in our school who studied so hard that he skipped a grade. He was voted president of his overwhelmingly white high school class, and then attended the local Baptist college. From there he went to medical school and became a prominent physician. This was before affirmative action.

He wanted to.

In graduate school, I held down three jobs while taking a full load of classes. One semester I put in thirty hours a week as an intern at IBM, served twenty hours a week as a university teaching assistant, and also worked part-time for a church. I earned straight A's as well.

I wanted to. I was poor, but I was going to better myself or die trying.

I'm all for improving education. As one who has suffered a bit, I'm also for helping anyone who's having a hard time. If you think I'm advocating that we be flinty toward the poor or slash public school budgets, then you misunderstand me.

Yet as Sharp and countless others in countless endeavors have shown us, we always need to remember—and to instill in the young—that it's not the school or the state or aid programs or even parents that determine how a student will turn out. Ultimately, the student decides.

THIS WEEK'S MEDITATION:

"Lord, help me to assume responsibility for myself and my actions. Help me do my best, whatever my limitations and however many times I may fail. I choose to strive for excellence in all that I do. I choose not to blame others for my shortcomings. I choose to act like an adult, even when I feel like a frightened child."

Last week we looked at how a little personal "want-to" can revolutionize a person's life and raise him or her above humble beginnings.

That's not the whole story, however.

Every idea must be held in balance. If we attribute all successes or failures solely to the efforts of the individuals involved, we're apt to glorify too lavishly those who do well and blame too unfeelingly those who languish.

The truth is, not all people are created in equal circumstances. A woman born into an aristocratic family of wealthy bankers likely will find it much easier to understand the principles of financial success, and earn a fortune of her own, than a woman of equal talent and energy born into a large, single-parent family living in an Appalachian trailer park. The latter woman might have to expend as much effort to earn a college degree at the nearest state university and find a job in middle management as the first needs to graduate from Yale, start her own corporation, and make millions of dollars.

So we should hesitate before judging others. We might not

know from whence they've risen. If we ourselves have had the opportunity to enjoy a measure of success, we should be humbly thankful.

When I'm discouraged about my own lot in life, when I've had a bad day at my writing or sour words with my wife, or, on the other hand, when I'm tempted to crow about some minor victory, I think back to my paternal grandfather, Fred Prather.

What a hard life he lived, and with so little reward.

He was born in 1895 into a family that was comparatively well off. His father was a teacher, a businessman, and a farmer. But when Papa was five his father died suddenly from dysentery. His mother, for reasons long since lost to time, couldn't manage her late husband's estate. Soon she and her children teetered on the edge of starvation.

By about the third grade, my grandfather was forced to quit school and go to work as a farm laborer. He once recalled in my presence the thrill he'd felt when his wages for a twelve-hour workday finally rose to a dollar a day.

Papa's mother became the kept woman of a prosperous neighbor. In those Victorian times, that quickly transformed her and her children into social outcasts. When young Fred Prather eventually wed my grandmother, Lennie Humble, the devout seventeen-year-old daughter of a landed farmer, her parents essentially disowned her for having married into such a family.

Not surprisingly, my grandparents' marriage turned unhappy. My grandmother spent much of her time regretting that she had bound herself to a semiliterate and socially unacceptable man. He groused that she should've married a rich preacher. Papa, who already had been an outcast much of his life, became nearly an outcast in his own home.

Papa's working life didn't improve much over the fifty or so years he spent in the labor force. During the Depression, when jobs were scarce as feathers on a boar, he tried to support five children by, among other things, pumping gas at someone else's service station. For twenty years after the Depression, he shoveled coal into the mouth of a blast furnace, sometimes six days a week, sixteen hours a day. That couldn't have left any time for him to educate himself or start his own business, even if he'd thought of such things. Whether or not he thought of them, I don't know.

Glimpses showed through—slivers of light, really—of another man. The one who might have been. Papa could be gentle. My dad says that when he was a child, the family walked to church because they couldn't afford to drive. In the winters my grandfather would scoop up Dad and carry him under his coat to keep him warm. In a place and age when fathers routinely beat their children with belts, straps, or sticks, Papa only spanked my dad once, when Daddy looked him in the eyes and flatly refused to do something Papa had asked him to. Papa was never a violent or hard-drinking man.

When I was a boy, I used to draw pictures. Once, I handed Papa my pencil and asked him to sketch a wagon I was having a hard time capturing on paper. To everyone's astonishment, he took the pencil and pad and drew an impressive likeness of the wagon.

As a teenager, I spent a week with my grandparents, helping

Papa paint his house because he was too old and weak to stand on a ladder all day. We passed evenings sitting beneath an apple tree. He told me tall tales, and we whooped with delight.

On another visit, he turned serious. "Son, stay in school," he said quietly after I'd told him I was considering skipping college. "I don't want you to have to work hard like I've always done."

Ultimately, I did eke out an education, thanks in part to that plea, and I landed a succession of jobs that all have seemed shamefully easy in comparison to his. I earn adequate wages. My wife loves me.

And so, as I said, I think about Papa when my lot seems bad or I'm tempted to sniff at those who haven't achieved even the paltry measure of success I've enjoyed. I wonder what Papa might have become had his father not died, had he grown up in the middle-class home his father would have provided rather than in a shack where public scorn seeped between the slats like a chilly rain.

I selfishly hoard my own good fortune. There are days I question by what justice, what divine logic, this orb of stone and mud revolves.

THIS WEEK'S MEDITATION:

"Let me be quick to kneel and thank You for the good fortune I've received. Let me be slow to judge those who have fared worse than I."

THE TEN RULES

I used to know a guy named Henry Darmstadter, an elderly Jewish man who ran a small barbecue restaurant. Darmstadter had seen a lot. He'd immigrated to America as a teen and had survived the Depression by working like a three-legged horse plowing a rocky field. As a U.S. soldier, he'd liberated fellow Jews from concentration camps.

Sometimes on Christmas Day, Darmstadter would open his restaurant to the homeless and feed hundreds free of charge. He took some kidding over that, he told me, a Jew feeding the hungry on Christmas.

"It's something that you feel like you want to do," he said, shrugging.

I admired him. So I asked him one day what principles guided him.

"I think that if you adhere by the Ten Commandments you can get along pretty good," he said.

That stuck in my mind.

Later, I interviewed former Kentucky lieutenant governor Steven Beshear for a newspaper story about religion and politics. When Beshear had run unsuccessfully for governor back in 1987, many Kentucky church groups had opposed him.

Partly, religious folks disliked him because he was pro-choice on the abortion issue. But there was another reason, too. Early in his political career, as state attorney general, Beshear had issued an opinion that removed the Ten Commandments from the walls of the Commonwealth's schools. That ruling was so volatile that, years after he'd issued it, it dogged his gubernatorial race.

Here we are, I thought, half a world and thousands of years removed from the day God supposedly handed Moses those stone tablets on Mount Sinai. But the Ten Commandments are very much with us. They affect the ways restaurant owners run their businesses and the ways voters choose their governors.

There's a reason for that: The commandments are eternal. They never were intended to be mere words chiseled into rocks. Instead, they were to be written on human hearts. At their core, the Ten Commandments are about showing respect to God and acting charitably toward others. They became the foundation of a comprehensive moral and social code that helped the Jewish community survive.

Maybe those ten rules don't belong on the walls of public schools. That's open for debate. Still, a new appreciation of the commandments would help salvage our troubled society. Over the next few weeks, we'll spend some time considering them.

THE FIRST COMMANDMENT:
"You shall have no other gods besides Me."

THE SECOND COMMANDMENT:
"You shall not make yourself a graven image. . . ."
EXODUS 20:3-6

During his short-lived Christian conversion, folk music icon Bob Dylan sang a song called "Gotta Serve Somebody." That song's message also is the premise of the Ten Commandments: Everybody serves somebody. As Dylan said, it may be the devil, or it may be the Lord. But you're going to live as someone's servant.

History shows that humans are unalterably religious. The question is not whether we'll worship but whether we'll worship properly. The first two commandments help focus our understanding on that eternal fact.

The Ten Commandments were written for ancient Jews who had escaped from centuries of slavery to brutal Pharaohs. The Bible prefaces the rules with this statement: "I am the Lord your God, who brought you out of the land of Egypt, out of the house of bondage." The commandments, by implication, are designed to ensure that the people remain free—by paradoxically enslaving them to the God of Abraham, Isaac, and Jacob, a gentle leader Who possesses the power to deliver them from all other masters.

But willingly choosing to serve another, even God, is a proposition that many people today find strange. They ask: "Why would we want to be slaves to anyone? We're already enlightened and liberated."

I don't think we're as free as we believe we are. All of us serve. Always have. The ancient Egyptians carved idols from wood or stone or gold. The commandments made it clear the Jews were no longer to bow down to those images.

Today, we're far too sophisticated to worship tree stumps. Or are we?

"The rigid Hebrew rule kept you from ornamenting your furniture, but it never kept you from worshiping your furniture," the late author and poet Joy Davidman wrote in *Smoke on the Mountain*, an examination of the Ten Commandments.

In short, even in contemporary life there are many potential "idols": antique tables, doctorates, cocaine, the U.S. presidency, Corvettes, the flag, the Lakers, sex, church services, the environment, stocks and bonds. Not that all these things are intrinsically evil. But anything to which we ascribe undue power, anything—no matter how good—to which we devote our lives at the cost of our relationship with the Almighty, can become our idol.

So we all have gods, even atheists. Most gods are the wrong ones.

Why do we worship them? Because we think we can control them, whereas the Judeo-Christian God demands to control us.

Control is a central obsession for us humans. In the Bible, humans' core problem, the basis of all sin from the Garden of Eden forward, is that we want to be in charge.

47

Idolatry, then, really is the worship of the self. If we can buy or make our idols, we can discard them when they no longer please us. If we can discard our gods, we are gods. And if we are gods, we can do whatever we wish.

The problem is that humans are incompetent and capricious deities. To quote Davidman again: "The modern materialist often makes it simply: 'Do what you like,' and then rushes off to ask his psychoanalyst why he no longer seems to like anything."

The message of the two initial commandments is that we aren't commandment makers; God is. We aren't the creators of the universe; we're merely creations.

The biblical question is not whether we will serve another; we will. The question is, Whom will we serve? The true Creator, Who even in our slavery to Him can liberate us toward justice and joy? Or false gods, driven by our self-love, who ultimately will leave us jaded and hollow?

THIS WEEK'S MEDITATION:

"Show me how to serve You, rather than myself."

WE HONOR GOD'S NAME, OURSELVES, OUR PARENTS

THE THIRD COMMANDMENT:
"Do not take the name of the Lord your God in vain. . . ."
EXODUS 20:7

When I was a child, teachers at Sunday school used to apply the third commandment mostly to cussing. But swearing in jest or anger is the least of the offenses we commit against God's name. The old Hebrew wording, translated here as taking God's name "in vain," meant far more than that. It also meant "in a tempest," "in devastation," "in evil," or "in uselessness."

The third commandment actually was saying, "Don't attach God's name to cruel actions that God doesn't have anything to do with." Religious folks are the worst abusers of that rule. Catholics and Protestants in Ireland invoke God's name before blowing up one another with bombs. In our country, says pastor and author John Killinger, we stamp "In God We Trust" on our coins, then put our trust in nuclear warheads.

TV evangelists use God's name to bilk money from Social Security recipients. Parents cite God's will to browbeat—and sometimes physically beat—their children.

Ominously, the third commandment adds this warning: ". . . for the Lord will not hold him guiltless who takes His name in vain." That's because the evil we commit in the name of God is the worst of all. In addition to hurting others, it slanders the Almighty.

THE FOURTH COMMANDMENT:
"Remember the Sabbath day, to keep it holy."
EXODUS 20:8

The fourth rule wasn't intended as an onerous burden on men and women, but actually as a guarantee of freedom and rest. For the ancient people of Israel, the Sabbath followed six long days of trudging beneath the desert sun. They needed one leisurely, tranquil day in which to recover from their efforts and refresh themselves.

The word "holy" in the ancient biblical languages mainly meant "set apart." When Moses ordered the Israelites to keep the Sabbath holy, he was saying that on this day they should rest instead of working, that they should take a little time to thank the God who offered them this time off—that this day should be spent differently than others.

It wasn't celebrated that way for long. Gradually, well-meaning religious folks transformed this divine gift into another excuse for stifling each other's joy. Jesus of Nazareth happened along more than a thousand years after the commandment originally had been given, and wasn't at all happy about how it then was being observed. In His day, by law you could only walk a short distance on the Sabbath. Religious leaders even criticized Jesus for healing the sick on the Sabbath. They reasoned that healing constituted a form of work—and all labor, even divine labor, was banned on that day.

An exasperated Jesus told them they'd misunderstood the spirit of the rule. "The Sabbath was made for man," he said. "Man wasn't made for the Sabbath." The day had been designed to lighten the loads of the ill and the weary. Instead, it had become an added weight.

Despite His admonition, for the better part of two millennia after He departed, even people who claimed to be devout followers of Jesus seemed not to have heard what He'd said about Sabbaths. When I was a boy, civil laws dictated that all but the most vital businesses must close on Sundays, when most Christians observed their Sabbaths. If a fellow even mowed his grass after attending Sunday morning church services, his neighbors gossiped about his sacrilege for the remainder of the week. Sabbath-breaking was serious business, in the eyes of the commonwealth and in the eyes of many of its citizens.

Now, that's all changed. If in Jesus' time, and in my own boyhood, the Sabbath was observed too stringently for comfort, currently it's hardly observed at all. Little League ball teams hold tournaments on both the Jewish and Christian Sabbaths. More and more, even in the Bible Belt, where I live, department stores offer sidewalk clothing sales.

The Sabbath nearly has faded from our society's consciousness. That's our loss. It never was meant as a legalistic imposition, but it was meant to be observed—as a day of rest and contemplation. Can you think of many things we need more than that?

THE FIFTH COMMANDMENT:
"Honor your father and your mother. . . ."
EXODUS 20:12

In the last weeks of my Grandmother Chestnut's life, as she withered from cancer in a hospital, she lost control of her bowels. Day after day, she suffered from an acidic diarrhea that left her raw and in pain.

Nurses cleaned her as best they could, but they had other patients with whom to deal. So my mom would go to the hospital, gently wash her mother's bottom—as in Mom's infancy Grandma had cleaned her—and then dry her with a hair dryer because Grandma was so sore she couldn't stand the touch of a towel.

That lowly act was the epitome of honoring your parents: showing them the same love and selfless devotion they have shown you.

But honoring your parents includes more than that. It's a way of life. It includes studying diligently, working hard, telling the truth, obeying the law, and supporting your children. It means conducting your life in such a manner that your parents feel honored to say: "That's my son. That's my daughter."

THIS WEEK'S MEDITATION:

"Help me understand that Your name is not a toy to be tossed around lightly. Help me recognize that I can ignore Your day of rest only at my own physical, mental, and spiritual peril. Help me show gratitude to my parents, who deserve honor for having given me life."

THE SIXTH COMMANDMENT:
"You shall not kill."
EXODUS 20:13

This commandment may be the most complex of all. Does it mean we should never take a human life under any circumstances? If so, what do we say to police officers who shoot armed bank robbers, or to bloodied marines who have destroyed an enemy's machine-gun nest? Must we all become pacifists?

Actually, Judeo-Christian thinkers long have recognized that because evil is unavoidable in our world, killing is at times a moral necessity.

The Hebrew word used in the commandment for "kill" does not condemn all violence. It's more like "murder," says the Reverend Earl F. Palmer in *Old Law—New Life*.

There are times when the evil act of killing one person can prevent the greater evil of, say, genocide. During World War II, even the peaceable German theologian Dietrich Bonhoeffer agreed that Hitler needed to be eliminated. Bonhoeffer participated in an unsuccessful plot to assassinate the dictator, for which he paid with his own life.

Really, the sixth commandment is concerned about the state of the killer's heart, before and after the deadly deed is committed. It says we're never to seek sheer vengeance, particularly as individuals taking the law into our own hands. We're never to kill for the animal thrill of it. We're never to allow ourselves to despise another person, no matter how despicable he might be; Jesus interpreted the sixth commandment to mean that bitterness and ill will were tantamount to murder, even if we didn't physically harm our adversaries.

There's a great irony here: Killing at times is justifiable, but it should never result from malice or recklessness or greed. It should never be taken lightly.

The late poet and author Joy Davidman wrote about an incident that followed the dropping of the atomic bomb on Hiroshima. To their own dismay, the U.S. airmen who flew that mission quickly were transformed into celebrities by the military establishment and the press. A Washington, D.C., socialite happily presented them with a cake in the shape of a mushroom cloud. A photograph of the cake was widely reprinted.

The nation was outraged. "No matter what we were—pacifist or militarist, civilian or soldier, Red or Red-baiter—we all hated that cake," Davidman recalled. Americans never agreed on whether the Hiroshima bombing was necessary: "But one thing we'll agree to: Necessary or not, it wasn't funny."

That agreement sprang from a national conscience formed

partly by the sixth commandment, she said. Davidman, however, was writing more than four decades ago. You have to wonder sometimes how much of that national conscience remains.

During the Gulf War, General Charles Horner showed graphic videotape of U.S. bombs slamming into the headquarters of his Iraqi counterpart. America collectively chuckled. In fact, many of us seemed to treat the whole war as if it were a big video game. If we ever realized that homes were being flattened to rubble, that legs and fingers and brains were being blasted away—well, we certainly didn't dwell on it.

That also violates the sixth commandment. Killing should remain repugnant. When we cheer the deaths of others, we've crossed a line.

No matter the justification for killing, it always diminishes the souls of the killers themselves. Lieutenant Colonel Dave Grossman, a U.S. Army psychologist, has spent years studying the impact upon normal men of having taken the lives of others in official military actions. In his book *On Killing* he makes a compelling argument that within the vast majority of us abides a deep, seemingly inborn resistance to killing.

Sadly, those who do kill—particularly those who dispatch their enemies at close range by shooting them with rifles or bayoneting them—often never recover from the experience. They're prone to nightmares, guilt, depression, alcoholism, suicide.

The catalyst for Grossman's research was the pioneering work of U.S. Army Brigadier General S. L. A. Marshall. While conducting after-battle interviews with troops during World War II,

Marshall made an astonishing discovery: In combat, only 15 to 20 percent of all American infantry soldiers had fired their weapons at the enemy.

The remaining 80 to 85 percent simply had declined to shoot at others, even when the enemy was attacking them. They had fired into the air, or into the ground, or had not fired at all.

Further research determined that the 15 to 20 percent fire rate held true for other armies as well, not just for Americans. More studies estimated that the tiny percentage of soldiers willing to kill had remained constant through previous wars, across the centuries.

After these startling findings, the U.S. military set out to improve the combat firing rate of its soldiers. What followed was a revolution in training methods. Five years later, in the fire-fights of the Korean War, 50 percent of American infantry troops were shooting at the enemy. By Vietnam, the figure was 90 percent.

The military succeeded by learning to temporarily short-circuit its soldiers' consciences. It made killing a conditioned response. The combat killing rate multiplied.

Other things multiplied alongside it, though, including the rate of psychological casualties and the frequency of atrocities committed by Americans against civilians.

Up to 54 percent of the 2.8 million military personnel who served in Vietnam fell victim to post-traumatic stress disorder, a far higher rate than in previous wars. Several factors contributed to this epidemic, but the central one was the increased percentage of soldiers struggling with the results of having killed. And the same training methods that made it easier to shoot enemy soldiers also made it easier for troops at My Lai and other places to slaughter women and children.

The question, then, Grossman says, is whether the increased efficiency in battle is worth the psychological cost to the soldiers who represent us, and to society itself.

Whenever one person takes another's life, even when the killing is justified by our culture, there can be no real victors. The "winner" loses, too.

THIS WEEK'S MEDITATION:

"Please remove from me the egotism, self-righteousness, and greed that produce hatred—because hatred is the highway on which murder travels. Let me be one who offers new life to others, not one who takes life away."

THE REMAINING
RULES OF LOVE

THE SEVENTH COMMANDMENT:
"You shall not commit adultery."

EXODUS 20:14

Strictly speaking, adultery is sexual intercourse between a married person and someone other than that person's spouse.

Rabbi Eric Slaton, a thoughtful acquaintance of mine, once told me that for the ancient Israelites a suspicion of adultery may have been even more damning than a suspicion of murder. The book of Numbers, for instance, provided an elaborate test to determine whether a suspected adulterer actually was guilty. Unfortunately, Slaton said, a double standard existed: Typically, only women were tested. Still, the point is, none of the other commandments included such a test.

Adultery was considered so serious because it destroyed the trust that was the cornerstone of a marriage. Marriage, in turn, was the cornerstone of the family. And the family was the cornerstone of society. So whatever tore up families was a threat to everyone, not just to the husbands and wives involved.

Interestingly, some modern writers have argued that adultery—unlike premarital sex—rarely is the momentary result of raging hormones or an overpowering infatuation. Just the opposite.

"Adultery is the sin of abandonment, of loss of interest, of rejection, of self-pity," writes the Reverend Earl F. Palmer in *Old Law—New Life*. "Most adultery is not at all like the highly charged carelessness of the young. . . . Instead, adultery is too often the desperate act of those who have gone stale in the afternoon of their lives and are feeling sorry for themselves because they are unhappy."

THE EIGHTH COMMANDMENT:
"You shall not steal."
EXODUS 20:15

Just before Christmas, I used a lunch hour to buy stocking stuffers for my wife. No sooner had I entered a knickknack store than I noticed a sales clerk following me. Every time I browsed up an aisle, there was the clerk, pretending to dust shelves or rearrange merchandise—while really watching me out of the corner of an eye. I was dressed reasonably well. I wasn't skulking around. I've never stolen anything in my adult life. But suddenly I felt guilty. And angry.

That's one of the results of theft: Like adultery, it destroys our ability to trust. Because a few people are crooks, everyone is a suspect.

"We have become a civilization of locks and bolts and security systems," one minister observed.

We often focus our outrage over thievery on hapless street muggers and shoplifters. They're only the least subtle robbers. Poet Joy Davidman said that any attempt to gain something for nothing is a form of thievery: "The thief is not only he who steals my purse but also he who steals my trade; and he who underpays me, and he who overcharges me; and he who taxes me for his own advantage instead of mine; and he who sells me trash instead of honest goods."

THE NINTH COMMANDMENT:
"You shall not give false testimony against your neighbor."
EXODUS 20:16

Truth is the basis of social and legal justice. The ninth rule primarily is a law against perjury—among the most ancient of prohibitions.

The Israelite commandment was a reflection of far older laws, Davidman wrote.

"Primitive men who killed and raped and looted without a second thought regarded a false oath as an offense against the gods and looked with superstitious horror for a bolt of lightning to strike the blasphemer dead," she said in *Smoke on the Mountain*. Babylonian and Roman legal codes made perjury a capital offense. A thief could steal his neighbor's horse, but a liar could rob him of his freedom and possibly his life, things more precious than material possessions.

As many religious thinkers have observed, there also are more subtle means for damning people with false words than courtroom lying. There's the slander of whispered gossip based on half-truths or mere supposition. That may not threaten people's lives or their freedom, but it certainly can destroy their reputations and their spirits.

THE TENTH COMMANDMENT:
"You shall not covet your neighbor's house . . .
or anything that is your neighbor's."
EXODUS 20:17

The last commandment has to do with contentment, the peace of mind that everyone really is seeking. It suggests that much of our unhappiness results from our wanting things we don't have: a better-paying job, a bigger house, a faster car, a more attractive spouse. Things our neighbor has.

Our economic system is based on the assumption that, no matter what we have, we always need more. Much advertising is about creating the belief in people that they need things they don't. The result is that most people, no matter how comfortable they should be, always remain dissatisfied. The result of dissatisfaction is that we constantly torture the earth to take more of its natural goods than necessary. Even though food and resources exist for everyone, we hoard. Some people end up with far too much; others are left to starve.

The last commandment warns that greed opens a maw that never is filled. As Saint Paul said, assuming we have clothes to wear and enough to eat—we should be happy.

A final thought about the Ten Commandments. Rabbi Norman D. Hirsh once said that they begin with the most abstract of ideas, about "the invisible God Who cannot be made visible." They end with the most concrete of images, about the sanctity of a neighbor's possessions. Similarly, in the Christian tradition, Jesus is quoted as saying that all God's laws can be summed up in two statements: Love the Lord with all your heart and love your neighbor as yourself.

The commandments tell us that our relationship with God is inseparable from our respect for our fellow humans. A person who honors God can't steal his friend's wife.

THIS WEEK'S MEDITATION:

"I choose to respect that which belongs to my neighbor, not only through my actions but by my words and in my very heart. And with Your help, I'll practice being content today with what I have today. In doing these things, I'll be truly honoring You."

THE MAJESTIC STORY OF PASSOVER

The story behind the Jewish observance of Passover is puzzling, bloody, and majestic. We'd do well to ponder it, for it reveals a great deal about God's personality—and His complexity.

Passover falls in March or April. It begins on the evening of each fourteenth of Nisan, the first month of the 360-day Jewish calendar. The original Passover took place in Egypt several thousand years ago. As Exodus tells it, the people called Israel had been enslaved there four hundred years, bound to a land ruled by a despotic Pharaoh.

Before the Israelites fell into bondage, God had promised their ancestor Abraham that his descendants always would remain God's chosen people. Yet across four centuries as servants in a foreign land, no deliverance had arrived for them.

Then one day Moses stalked into the Israelites' midst. For the forty previous years he'd been herding sheep in an obscure wilderness. Eighty years old and always hampered by a "slow tongue," Moses nevertheless announced to his Hebrew brothers and to Pharaoh's court alike that God had sent him to deliver Abraham's descendants.

Both groups scoffed at the eccentric old man. At least they scoffed until Moses performed a series of supernatural feats that backed up his claims. He called down plagues from heaven on the Egyptians.

Repeatedly, Pharaoh refused to release the slaves. They were too many—perhaps two million—and too valuable. Besides, Pharaoh didn't want to admit defeat.

So Moses made one final, incredible pronouncement: God's angel of death would pass through Egypt. As retaliation for Pharaoh's stubbornness, the angel would kill the firstborn of every household in the land, from the eldest of Pharaoh's children to the eldest child of servant girls to the firstborn among cattle.

The Israelites alone would be spared this awful curse. But to escape the plague—and Egypt—they must follow Moses' instructions exactly. Every head of a Jewish household must choose an unblemished lamb from his flock. On the evening of the fourteenth of Nisan he was to kill the animal, then daub its blood on the doorposts and lintel of his house. The Lord God had told Moses this: "The blood will be a sign for you on the houses where you dwell; and when I see the blood, I will pass over you. No plague will destroy you when I strike Egypt."

After sacrificing the animals and sprinkling their blood, the Jews were to roast the lambs that same night and eat the mutton inside their houses, with bitter herbs and unleavened bread. Moses commanded the people to carry out this ritual while fully dressed, with their sandals on and staffs in their hands. They would need to flee quickly.

The Israelites did as they were told. After midnight on the fifteenth of Nisan, they heard terrible weeping. Throughout Egypt, people and animals lay dead. None of the Israelites had died, though.

Pharaoh summoned Moses and his brother Aaron in the darkness. He told them to take their people and leave Egypt. The rattled king let the slaves depart with flocks of sheep, herds of cattle, and gold. He just wanted to be rid of them.

This deliverance was so awesome that Moses, prodded by God, commanded that it should be remembered each year among the Jews, forever.

Subsequent generations reverently have celebrated the Passover as if they themselves had been delivered "out of bondage to freedom, from sorrow to gladness, and from mourning to festival day, and from darkness to great light, and from servitude to redemption," as the code of the ancient rabbis, the Mishnah, describes it.

But the story is a bloody one that can offend contemporary sensibilities. Why, we might ask, would God kill innocent Egyptian children? If somebody needed to die for the slaves to go free, why didn't God just kill Pharaoh, the evil taskmaster? Why did He order the Israelites to slaughter thousands of harmless lambs?

For many Jews and Christians, there's also the issue of the numerous miracles and plagues in the Exodus account. Are we to believe they occurred literally? If so, how do we explain them in scientific terms? Or should we consider the whole story as merely a religious fable?

Frankly, I don't know all the answers to such questions.

But to dwell disproportionately on them, I think, is to miss the Passover's greater glory, a series of revelations the Bible makes about God's very nature.

First, in the Passover we see a God Who doesn't much regard earthly social status. He clearly prefers a tribe of slaves to the Pharaoh's grandeur. He chooses as His spokesman an elderly sheep farmer who suffers from a speech disability.

Second, we're shown a God who keeps His promises. He has sworn to deliver Abraham's seed and make them His own children and a mighty nation. He does just that, although it takes Him centuries longer to act than the Israelites might have preferred.

Third, we find a God Who loves those children jealously. Like an angry Father, He fights viciously to rescue them.

Fourth, we encounter a God who "passes over" His people's sins. He delivers them despite their innumerable flaws (which become all too evident as the Exodus account progresses).

Fifth, we see that in God's economy, salvation for one person or nation can sometimes be purchased by the sacrificial blood of another party. The lambs, in their deaths, spare the Israelites. For Christians—I hope my Jewish friends will forgive me here—Passover's slain sheep foreshadow the redemptive death of Jesus.

Finally, we see a God glad to free those who can't free themselves.

Passover then is, as much as anything, a tale of God's redemptive grace. He's a complicated being, but He loves extravagantly and jealously those who are His.

THIS WEEK'S MEDITATION:

"Dear God, remembering Passover, I will celebrate the various ways in which You have passed over my sins, delivered me from slavery, and pointed my feet toward the Promised Land."

RESURRECTION MERCY

For serious Christians, it's not Christmas but Easter that's the holiest day of the year. More remarkable than the thought that God could be born as a human baby is that He died in disgrace, lay in a grave three days—long enough for his corpse to stink— and then returned to life, revived by a power so explosive it blew the massive stone off His tomb's doorway.

The resurrection's explicit promise is this: Death isn't the end. If Christ conquered His own grave, then He holds the power to someday raise as well those who have trusted Him. Life in this present age can be mean and always is brief, but the resurrected ones' afterlife with Jesus is good and lasts forever.

Still, if Christians are right, even if Jesus plans to resurrect us, too, we might ask ourselves why He would bother. After all, Jesus lived a sinless life; the morals of His disciples leave much to be desired. He remained faithful to God; we daily prove ourselves faithless. He's now seated in glory; we are dust. Why would He want to spend eternity with the likes of us?

Well, admittedly it's difficult to read God's mind. But there's a poignant clue in the biblical accounts of the original Easter. Each of the four gospels—Matthew, Mark, Luke, and John—tells the story a bit differently, as you would expect when four writers recount an event for four different audiences several decades after the fact.

Generally, they agree that a group of women, among them a certain Mary Magdalene, had gone early that Sunday morning to the graveyard. There, they found that the massive stone placed as a seal to Jesus' cavelike tomb already had been displaced. One or more of the women entered the tomb. The body was missing. The women's initial thought was that enemies had stolen His remains.

At some point—the texts disagree—one or two luminous angels appeared before the startled women and announced that Jesus was very much alive. Most of the women rushed to carry this news to the other disciples. No one knew quite what to make of it all.

But here John adds something. John says that, after everyone else had examined the tomb and returned home, Mary Magdalene remained, weeping and confused.

In her agony, she peered again into the sepulchre. Suddenly she saw two men dressed in dazzling white sitting on the empty shelf where Jesus' body had lain. Mary Magdalene pivoted, likely preparing to flee. As she turned, she found herself facing a third man dressed in ordinary work clothes, whom she took to be the gardener.

"Why are you crying?" he asked.

"Sir," she sobbed, "if you've taken away the body, please tell me where it is and I'll bring it back."

The gardener said, "Mary!"

Hearing her name, Mary Magdalene suddenly recognized—Jesus.

She gasped, "Teacher!" and grabbed him in a hug that must have popped His spine, assuming His resurrected body had one.

"Stop clinging to Me," Jesus said at last. "I haven't yet gone to see my Father."

So Mary Magdalene released Him and sprinted away to proclaim the resurrection, the first eyewitness to a risen Savior.

We don't know a lot about Mary Magdalene, except that she'd led a troubled life. Mark says that Jesus previously had exorcised seven demons from her. If you've seen *The Exorcist*, you can imagine that a woman possessed by seven devils would be tough to deal with—at least until Jesus set her free. Her reputation must have been awful.

Some traditions have it that Mary Magdalene also was a prostitute. Others speculate that she traveled among the rich women who apparently followed Jesus from town to town, contributing to His support. In either case, she must not have been emotionally bound to a husband or children.

In that light, think of the paradox in this little tale-within-a-tale.

It's the morning of the greatest event in history. The Creator of the universe has waged war with Satan and won. Jesus bursts forth from the tomb amid a heaven-sent earthquake. He's destined to ascend into heaven and sit on a throne at God's right hand. He's established forever as the Alpha and Omega, the Son of God, the Eternal Prince.

Here's what He doesn't do first. He doesn't go see His heavenly Father. He doesn't appear before His earthly mother, Mary, who birthed Him and nurtured Him. He doesn't show Himself to the apostles. He doesn't strike down Caiaphas the high priest or Pilate the Roman governor, the men responsible for His wrongful execution. He doesn't materialize before Caesar in Rome and demand that the ruler of the civilized world bow to a greater Emperor. He doesn't clothe Himself in eye-searing splendor, surrounded with fire and trumpet blasts.

No. The first thing Jesus does is dress as a working man and walk over to talk with Mary Magdalene. She's a mere woman in an age when women essentially are treated as livestock. She's a troubled person with a bad reputation, maybe even a hooker.

But Jesus chooses to reveal His resurrection first to her. It's an act of quiet love, one not necessarily logical. Love frequently overpowers logic.

What does this tell us?

Like His father, it seems, Jesus cares passionately and tenderly about His creation. He's concerned when Peter doesn't catch enough fish or a crowd needs its supper. It's as simple, and as unfathomably profound, as that. He first reveals himself to Mary Magdalene because she's there and she's hurting and she's His.

She's of no consequence to the Pilates of the world. She's flawed and fallen. But Jesus loves her. He longs to see her laugh more than He wants to claim His rightful glory in heaven. He wants to fill the dark tomb in her heart with an eternal light.

We can trust such a Lord to resurrect us.

THIS WEEK'S MEDITATION:

"Dear Lord, shed Your resurrection light in my heart. Lead me to life, now and in the age to come. Amen."

MEETING HEAVEN'S
WELCOMING COMMITTEE

I remember hearing my dad's mom, Lennie Prather, tell about the death long ago of her own mother. Country people still died at home in those days, rather than in hospitals or nursing homes. My Granny Prather had hovered with her sisters around their mother's sickbed in their family's old farmhouse, awaiting the inevitable.

Suddenly my great-grandmother lifted her head.

"Do you hear that?" she asked her daughters.

"Hear what, Mother?" one said.

"That beautiful singing."

The daughters all fell silent, listening.

"You can't hear that music?" their mother said. "It's so beautiful. Can't you see the angels? Why, they're coming for me."

And with those words, or similar ones, my great-grandmother lay her head back on her pillow and died, peacefully.

Whether she truly saw angels entering her room or experienced a hallucination brought on by the final shutting down of her brain is open to debate.

But my Granny Prather had no doubts. She was certain that angels had come to escort her mother into the heaven about which their Baptist faith spoke often, a blissful land of angels and halos.

Even today statistics show that the vast majority of Americans believe in some kind of heaven. Its specifics depend upon whom you ask. A seminary scholar once suggested to me that it's similar to the earth, but with the suffering removed. He said heaven's citizens can grow, learn, and work, just as people do now. The Revelation of John describes heaven as a walled city with twelve gates and streets of pure gold. Methodism's founder, John Wesley, taught that people's favorite pets would be there; dogs and cats might even have the power to speak with us.

No one knows what heaven is like except those who already have entered its gates, and they're not telling. But belief in a paradise is a great comfort to the dying. Clergy who work with the terminally ill tell me that people who've lived deeply religious lives face the end more calmly than those who wrestle with spiritual uncertainty. In the days or weeks before they die, many religious folks report seeing visions of Jesus or deceased loved ones.

"It's like people who are [devout] have a reception committee waiting for them," said a minister I know who counsels cancer patients at a university hospital. He isn't certain what to make of these stories. They might be figments created by brain chemicals. Or, he said, as folks draw nearer to death "their spiritual eyes may be opened."

I hope the visions are real, that heaven is like the best parts of the earth we've experienced, and that we'll get a second chance to revisit what we've loved here.

Not so long ago, I went down to Pulaski County, Kentucky, to what's left of the farm where my family lived nearly one hundred years. The farm as I knew it exists no more. After my maternal grandfather, Oscar Chestnut, died in 1968, my grandmother couldn't keep up the land. She sold it to a real-estate developer, saving only her clapboard home and an acre of ground. For fifteen more years the farm continued to look much as it had since Oscar's father, my Great-grandpa Lee Chestnut, cleared it from forest in the 1890s. The developer who had bought the farm kept the fields mowed and grazed cattle on them.

Then, at last, the developer began to develop. Now a low-slung bungalow leers at me from under the farm's biggest maple tree. I remember when a log-and-plank cabin sat near the same spot, the cabin where my great-grandfather first moved his young bride a century ago, the cabin where my grandfather was born.

The barn lot my grandfather used to cross as he returned from milking his cows is today the yard of a tidy split-level house. A modified Cape Cod sits where the large garden was. My grandfather used to take me on tractor rides there. Unbelievably, my grandfather now has been buried thirty years. My son is older than I was when Papa died. Grandma Chestnut died in 1986.

Only the clapboard main house remains, along with a couple of outbuildings. It was built in 1914, after the Chestnut family outgrew its cabin and improved its meager fortunes. Strangers own it now. Except for the old house, our family's farm is just one more of those characterless subdivisions that blight the nation, pattern-cut homes baking treelessly in the sun.

It seems it's been only a couple of weeks since I was a kid, hunting in the unblemished fields of the Chestnut farm, a shotgun under my arm, as my ancestors had. Then I blinked, and I was a middle-aged man with eyeglasses, a waistline bigger than my chest, and a mortgage. The fields were gone. Most of my family was lost as well.

For that matter, the entire Oak Hill community that I remember is lost. After my Great-aunt Marie passed away, her country store was burned as a training exercise for local firefighters. Its sagging porch and brick-patterned tar paper, and decades of Marie's life and sweat, were whisked away in a few hours' blaze, smoke, and, finally, embers. My mother's two-room school was torn down long before that.

Any effort to stop time is merely vanity and striving after wind. That's part of what ultimately pushes people to God, I suspect, that moment when we recognize the crushing truth: Nothing lasts. Religion is a groping effort to transcend that oblivion. In churches, in synagogues, in mosques, in Buddhist meditation groups, everyone is searching for the same thing. A way to break the clock, or at least to turn it back.

I don't know what heaven's like, but it pleases me to think of it that way. For me, heaven is where the barn from my childhood still stands. It's where my grandfather walks toward me across a grassy lot, smiling, lugging his full milk buckets. It's where my son will always be a towheaded boy, leaping happily toward my outstretched arms. It's where I'll be allowed to savor the sweetness of each new day before it has disappeared, and where I can reclaim the countless days I've lost.

THIS WEEK'S MEDITATION:

"Lord, I'm sure Your design of heaven surpasses anything I could plan. Help me to live so as to attain it when I leave this place. And allow me then to behold not only Your glorious future but also the better portions of my past."

WHAT IS HELL LIKE?

There was an era when churches almost overdosed on the subject of hell. When I was a kid in the Bible Belt, it seemed as if every other Sunday the sermon was either about the terrible Second Coming of Jesus or the tortures of Hades.

Often it was on both, if the preacher could work both topics into a single message and still get us out of church by noon, before people's attention started wandering from the fiery pits of perdition and toward fried chicken and mashed potatoes.

But if ministers back then spent too much time expounding on hell, they've mostly gone too far in the other direction today. You hardly hear about it from many pulpits. Acknowledging the doctrine of damnation is a bit embarrassing to some clergy now, sort of like having to introduce your suave new friends to your Uncle Tex, who chews tobacco and lets the juice drool around his one tooth onto his polka-dotted polyester shirt.

The nearly total absence of hell from religious messages is at least an unfortunate oversight and possibly an eternal disservice. Browse through the New Testament and you'll find that Jesus and His disciples had at least as much to say about damnation as about salvation. They staunchly believed Hades was a real place.

In earlier centuries many artists drew, etched, or painted their visions of hell, and writers similarly produced a massive body of literature about it.

Interestingly, opinion surveys consistently show that the great majority of American laypeople continue to agree with Jesus and his friends on the subject. For instance, a Time/CNN/Yankelovich poll found that 73 percent of Americans believe in hell, 23 percent don't believe, and 4 percent aren't sure.

Ultimately, hell must exist if God has truly given humans free will, a Catholic priest once told me.

"God leaves us free to love Him or not," he said. "God doesn't force His love upon us. That's what hell basically says. It's not that God's punishing us, but that if we choose to reject God's love, God won't force us to love Him because that's not love."

Scholars say the concept of hell gradually grew out of Jewish and Greco-Roman observations that earthly justice was ineffective.

Christians later elaborated on the idea. Today, Christian traditionalists believe the unredeemed are tortured in a lake of fire, as the New Testament maintains. The damned are eaten by worms and confined to darkness. The most horrible thing is that once they're in hell, they can neither repent nor die.

Others understand Hades not as a place of literal fire, but nevertheless as a place of awful mental anguish. They say that people who have decisively and intentionally rejected God in this life have in essence rejected love. Such unhappy folks lead lives here marked by bitterness, strife, and recriminations. Their hell is to spend eternity in the company of other like-minded people—as well as with Satan.

Another Catholic priest described hell to me as a place where God is absent. Death is merely a blip in a spiritual cycle that begins on the earth, he said. Those who love God here will continue to love Him more fully in the afterlife; those who reject God here will be separated from Him totally in the world to come.

"Death is like a theological hiccup," the priest said.

Hell, then, we might speculate, is where God finally gives those who have refused to obey Him exactly what they want—a place away from His presence.

Really I doubt that it's necessary for God to torture the souls in such a place. The worst punishment would be for Him to abandon them to their own devices. The Bible says plainly who the citizens of hell will be: Satan and his fallen angels; the Beast of Revelation and his evil false prophet; people who worshiped the Beast; rebels; murderers; thieves; cowards; sorcerers; drug abusers; idolaters; liars; sexual perverts; the violent and unforgiving.

The worst thing about hell is your neighbors. Satan and his cronies run the place. The guy next door on one side might be from Rwanda, where he hacked all his rivals to death with a machete. On the other side of you lives a child molester. Across the street is a family of thieving crack heads.

Hell is like a modern-day maximum-security prison—except there are no guards to protect you from the other inmates. There are no civil rights. There's no safety at all, because God has withdrawn His protective, restraining hand.

It's a kingdom utterly "free" from God's love and God's rules. Consequently it's filled with millions of humans and demons twisted by every imaginable sin. The residents all chose to ignore God while in this world. He ignores them in the next.

Everybody there tells lies and speaks nothing but wickedness. You're constantly confused. Everybody's up to no good. Everybody wants to hurt you, and there's no justice when they succeed. Nobody cares about you. Everyone's gloomy. Everyone's depressed. It's always dark. People growl with anger and moan in fear.

Perhaps the worst torture in such a place would be realizing how easily you could have avoided your sentence if you hadn't been so hardheaded. You'd remember your little old grandmother who begged you to obey the Lord, the street evangelist who handed you a religious tract—and how you sneered at them.

THIS WEEK'S MEDITATION:

"Help me live productively, humbly, and circumspectly, as if my being condemned to hell were a real possibility; and by Your grace grant me reprieve from that terrible place if it is."

CHURCH IS INDEED A PLACE FOR HYPOCRITES

Frequently, out of curiosity, I ask former churchgoers why they quit. One answer I hear is that there are too many hypocrites in organized religion. It's a pretty good answer, as excuses go. The hypocrisy in churches bothers me, too.

I remember a congregational song leader from my boyhood, a local businessman in the town where we then lived, who would stand behind the pulpit and sing piously, his eyes turned toward heaven. Between songs he would talk on and on about how close he and Jesus were, about how much he liked to pray and feel the Lord's presence, about how many blessings God had bestowed upon him.

Unfortunately, his Sunday friendship with the Lord didn't stop him during the week from cheating on his wife or from brokering crooked financial deals.

Even as a kid that bugged me. I couldn't figure out why a fellow with so few discernible morals would masquerade as a devout Christian. It didn't profit him in his business, I don't think. Everybody knew what he really was like. So why not go on and admit that he was a heathen? Then he could have dispensed with getting up early on Sunday mornings and struggling into a suit and tie.

But then I got older, and I made a few discoveries about life and faith.

First, I realized that a great many churchgoers aren't such stark hypocrites. Most parishioners are sincere in their beliefs and genuinely try, at least, to live up to the codes they profess.

I've seen men stay in troubled marriages because they put the sanctity of their wedding vows before their personal happiness. I've seen women risk their jobs by refusing to take part in morally questionable deals. I've seen people sacrifice promising careers to spend more time with their children.

Second, I realized that hypocrisy isn't so much a church problem as a human problem. People of all stripes say one thing and do another.

A hypocrite is a liberal who preaches tolerance toward every imaginable point of view—except the views of conservatives who disagree with him. A hypocrite is a conservative who extols "family values" to his neighbors, then treats his children like hedgehogs. A hypocrite is a civic-minded business executive who cuts costs by slashing the jobs of his hourly workers, then accepts a massive bonus for his fine performance and praise for his generous contributions to some trendy charity.

A hypocrite is anyone who gossips about a coworker's being a gossip. A hypocrite is a mother who lectures her daughter on the evils of drugs while sucking on a cigarette and downing a whiskey sour.

Politics, of course, is full of hypocrisy. As I write this, President Clinton has been impeached by the House of Representatives for engaging in an extramarital affair with a White House intern half his age and then lying about it. The most powerful man in the world, a champion of women's rights, used his office as the country's CEO to hit on a lowly worker young enough to be his daughter; the man sworn to uphold law, truth, and justice apparently misled a grand jury and lied to the public that elected him. A hypocrite.

He found himself excoriated by House Republicans. Then, in the midst of the brouhaha, several of these same members of Congress were forced to admit that, yes, they too had engaged in extramarital affairs. Hypocrites all.

I list myself among the hypocritical ranks.

Not long ago, I preached a forceful Sunday sermon against the sin of grumbling. I hate it when people constantly complain and look for the negative in every situation. If you believe the Bible, God hates that, too. The Old Testament says God once killed fifteen thousand people in one swoop just because they grumbled.

The day after my sermon—the very next day!—I got a phone call from a woman who told me some unpleasant news about a church matter that I'd been trying to reconcile. I spent the rest of the afternoon fuming and railing about the situation. I grumbled and then grumbled some more—the very thing I'd just preached against.

Worried about seeing a hypocrite? Don't look in the mirror.

Because, sadly, most of us are hypocrites to one extent or another. Pretending not to be one might be the worst form of hypocrisy.

Maybe that's where churches get into trouble. Most churchgoers I know are all too aware of their own shortcomings. And still, for some reason, their message sounds to outsiders like this: "Hey, we don't have any flaws. It's you others who are messed up."

Those "others" know better. That's why they get offended.

What churches ought to say, and say outright, is: "Yeah we probably are, like you, hypocrites. But please bear with us. We know we're hypocrites. And we're working on it."

Hypocrisy is among the most insidious of human sins. But churches were made for sinners. That's why we're supposed to worship God and not worship church members. If church people were flawless, they wouldn't need God.

So if churches take in drunks and losers and ex-cons and prostitutes—and they should, as those are the people to whom the Founder ministered—then why shouldn't they open their doors to hypocrites as well? As someone said, a church is a spiritual hospital for damaged souls. That includes the souls of hypocrites.

You should never allow your fear that the pews will be packed with hypocrites keep you from attending your local church or temple. There's always room for one more.

> ### THIS WEEK'S MEDITATION:
>
> *"Let me see my own hypocrisy—so that I won't be so critical of others'. Mature me, Lord, to understand that even good people can exhibit flaws. We're all messed up. That's why we need You."*

WHY DO RELIGIONS MAKE
THOSE NETTLING LAWS?

A couple of my friends were discussing a play one of them had seen. Its characters had included a Mormon woman whose religion taught her that smoking cigarettes was sinful. In the play, this character would sneak a drag from someone else's cigarette, then cringe, afraid her nosy Mormon neighbors might see her.

That's just the problem with religion, my friends groused. It heaps guilt on some people for minor peccadilloes such as smoking and turns others into snoops.

"Oh," I said, "I think that's among the most valuable things religion does."

My pals looked at me, aghast.

I'm not a Mormon and my faith doesn't condemn cigarettes. I'm a grandson of tobacco farmers. My rural church sits on a hillside surrounded by tobacco fields.

Still, like many religious rules, this antismoking edict seems to me pragmatic and beneficial for the play's character, her family, and society.

Just think about it. Our fictional Mormon's yearning for tobacco isn't curbed by her belief that smoking is wrong. But her religion does give her a strong incentive for not yielding to her temptation. Instead of smoking openly and perhaps devouring three packs a day, she ends up smoking clandestinely and feeling guilty about it. She consumes, let's say, three cigarettes a month.

One result is hypocrisy; she pretends not to crave the vice she clearly does crave. Another result is that her chances of developing emphysema or lung cancer are significantly lowered. She's less likely to die a slow expensive death at an early age, leaving her children and medical bills to the state. Her family isn't exposed to secondary smoke. I'd argue that when the balance sheet is tallied, her faith's no-smoking rule has done her, and us, a great good.

And that's what most legalistic religious rules were meant to do, back when people paid attention to them. They didn't make us perfect, and they did have a down side. Yet they also protected us, by curbing our natural and irresponsible hedonism.

Take the ancient prohibition against sex outside marriage, a tenet generally pooh-poohed today. Having ignored that law, we live in a land ravaged by epidemics. There's AIDS, which is partly the result of promiscuity. There are nearly twenty other sexually transmitted diseases as well; a quarter of Americans are infected, one recent study found. Add to that 1.4 million abortions a year, the emotional toll of divorces caused by extramarital affairs, and the economic cost of hundreds of thousands of births to single mothers—most of whom will rear their children in poverty. We'd all be better off if we reserved sex for the marriage bed.

It might not be awful if churches still encouraged a twinge of guilt among those who won't practice sexual self-control. Would guilt stop everyone from messing around? Only a moron would think so. It might stop some, though, and it would keep others from playing around as much.

Then there's the question of teetotaling Methodists and Baptists. It's easy to wonder how some Christian groups can be so critical of strong drink, considering that Jesus turned water into wine at parties and was, in his own words, known as "a gluttonous man, and a winebibber."

Even among congregations that preach abstention, lay members often wink at their ministers' dictums and go on. (A joke among my Baptist pals: "What's the Baptist idea of heaven?" Answer, "It's where we can speak to each other in the liquor store.")

Indeed, some groups known for temperance today used to imbibe freely. Old-time Baptist congregations frequently paid their ministers in jugs of liquor. Baptists slowly changed their minds, largely because of the social ills wrought by booze.

George Will has noted that in the pre–Civil War United States, "Americans commonly drank whiskey at breakfast and on through the day. Laborers digging the Erie Canal were given a quart of Monongahela whiskey a day, issued in eight four-ounce portions beginning at six A.M." Cities and farms alike were rife with workers too soused to perform their duties. Alcoholic men abandoned their families.

Temperance movements attempted to dam that tidal wave of

liquor. Prohibition, for instance, which lasted from 1920 to 1933, now is portrayed as a repressive period during which Americans were barred by religious zealots from enjoying themselves.

The facts are different. Prohibition didn't outlaw drinking; people could make and consume home brew. But it was designed to shut down bars and keep working men at home, to stop them from spending all their money at saloons while their families starved, Prohibition historian John C. Burnham of Ohio State University has written.

Prohibition was a mixed success. Alcoholism rates plummeted. Drying-out hospitals, common before World War I, disappeared. Overall, alcohol consumption fell by one-third to one-half. Despite common wisdom to the contrary, Prohibition didn't result in documentable increases in organized crime, according to Burnham.

If we're honest, we must admit that today alcoholism again ranks as our worst drug epidemic, with 15.1 million addicts. Alcohol-related causes kill 200,000 Americans yearly. The federal government estimates that 13 percent of adults will at some point abuse alcohol, whereas only 6 percent will abuse illegal drugs.

Long ago, certain churches recognized liquor's dangers. Some even said, "Hey, maybe it would just be better if no one drank—particularly Christians, who are supposed to set good examples." That's an extreme solution, but not an illogical one.

Critics point out, rightly, that not everyone needs religious dogmas to live a healthy, moral life. There are atheists who don't chase skirts or drink to excess, who are better people than your typical churchgoer. But even atheists, if they dig deeply, will find that their morality has been influenced by society's previous agreements that certain acts are wrong. Those agreements often can be traced directly to religion's influence.

Most religious rules are, at core, laws for abundant living, reflections of a wisdom refined over thousands of years.

Nothing comes free. The price we pay for promoting beneficial guidelines is a certain amount of unpleasantness: a dash of hypocrisy here, a tad of snoopiness there.

But ask yourself which you would rather endure: an annoying conscience or herpes? Snoopy neighbors or lung cancer?

THIS WEEK'S MEDITATION:

"Help me become wise enough to curb my appetites. Help me avoid the legalistic self-denial practiced by hypocrites and neurotics, while embracing the healthy moderation recommended by the sages."

A GREAT
DETERMINED WOMAN

I happened across my Granny Prather's handwritten autobiography a few years ago. It was buried in a drawer at my parents' house. I now keep it in the office in my home, the place where I do my own studying and writing. From time to time, when I feel I'm forgetting who I am or I'm losing my nerve, I take it out and reread a few pages.

"I am writing this as a testimony," it begins.

And that's what it is.

Granny's life story wouldn't mean much to literary critics. Her prose wasn't eloquent (and in her old age and final sickness her penmanship was worse). But reading silently, I hear her voice in the words. Words never left Lennie Prather's mouth by accident, or halfheartedly.

I was a teenager in 1974 when she came to stay with us because she was too feeble to go home. For years, she'd battled cancer.

First thing in the morning, she used to warble out old Baptist hymns in a timbre that, if discordant, was filled with intention. Hers was the joyful voice of a woman set free: free from a coma, free from a rest home, free from death.

It was while she was at our house that she undertook the "book" of her life's story. She wanted to leave her grandchildren a legacy, and she had no money. So Granny wrote us sixty-plus pages in longhand. It was a slow, physically painful project.

As far as I can recall, I'm the only one of her grandchildren who has read her autobiography. Some family members have expressed little interest in it, and others already were scattered to places such as California and Ohio by the time she wrote it, and perhaps don't even know it exists.

Granny was born near the turn of the century, the book says, "in the deep country" of Pulaski County, Kentucky, to a tenant farmer and his wife. She tells much: of her father, who raised himself from tenant farmer to landowner and law officer; of relatives from her youth who remembered the Civil War; of a real haunted house. With no medicines except "turpentine for stomachache, coal oil and lard for one thing and some other such remedies for something else," Granny nearly died as a child of typhoid fever.

But she persevered and returned to grammar school, which was held three months a year in a log schoolhouse, taught by a man "who was very strict and rude, who actually had no education."

Granny, you see, had two lusts.

Education was one. Her dream was to become a teacher. At seventeen, she married my grandfather, a semiliterate farmer, because he promised to put her through school. He didn't or couldn't. She always resented him for that. Theirs wasn't an easy relationship, as I noted in the earlier chapter about Papa Prather. From what I witnessed, Granny was mainly at fault. She never learned to abide what she viewed as his ignorance and lack of ambition and she wouldn't control her tongue. Stunted dreams can do bad things to a person.

I suppose Papa did give her an education of sorts, but not the kind she craved. He gave her five babies. When she realized that her own dream of teaching would never come to pass, she shifted her lust for knowledge to her children. She ultimately forced a move from the farm where she and Papa were sharecroppers to the city of Somerset so that her children, at least, could go to a decent school. My dad became the family's first college graduate and, among other things, a schoolteacher. For several years he even worked as an administrator at a small college.

Granny's other great lust was religion. She taught adult Sunday school classes for decades, and her memory of the Scripture was encyclopedic; preachers relied upon her as their breathing concordance. Both her sons became ordained ministers.

If her will was heroic, her body was small and sickly. Her last ailment was the cancer that brought her to live with us. By that time, she'd been given up for dead by her doctors but had lived. She'd lain in a coma and lost the use of her limbs. For a year, she'd been confined to a nursing home. There, after awakening from her coma, Granny had taught herself to scrawl her alphabet again and had mailed cards to her children telling them, in the script of a toddler, that she must go home. She would not die among strangers. She'd taught herself to walk on wobbling, atrophied legs. That's when my dad, her youngest child, brought her to our house.

Near the end of her story, composed with a hand that months before had been useless, Granny remembers standing up to a previous serious illness. She conquered that disease, she writes, for one reason: "For I am a great determined woman."

That sums up her life.

A page or two later, her handwritten autobiography stops abruptly in midsentence. She left it unfinished because she got a sudden opportunity to return to her small house in Somerset. Without hesitating, she went home, where she'd intended all along to go. Once again, she'd persevered against a tough adversary.

Death soon claimed her, but only on her terms. She died in her own bed, surrounded by her own walls, the way she meant to die.

Somehow the last page of her autobiography is appropriate. There's no end to the story. There's no end to her life.

Reading Granny's words, I always feel determination rise within me like a mountain creek overflowing its banks. I remember that I have a heritage of strength, and that victory is in my genes. It's what Granny intended when she laboriously wrote those pages.

That was her testimony, and her life. And both continue.

For me, there's an additional message in her story. I know from her example that even the most powerful will can't bend everyone and every circumstance to its course. Not all of Granny's children or grandchildren inherited her craving for learn-ing. Even fewer acquired her devotion to God. But her deter-mination influenced all of us, and helped a few of us, and that's more than would have happened had she not stood strong.

If her faults were many, so were her virtues. I'm grateful to her.

THIS WEEK'S MEDITATION:

"Lord, mold my will like steel—but also temper it like an arrowhead, so that it reaches its target without wounding the innocent people near its path."

How to Enjoy a
Happy Marriage

Considering that our choice of mates affects the rest of our lives, as well as our children's lives and our grandchildren's lives, it's amazing how little thought some people put into it beforehand.

And even those who do think ahead often need Herculean strength to solve the unforeseen problems that emerge after their vows have been spoken.

Renee and I have been married two decades. I've spent nearly that many years as a minister regularly counseling couples who are in one marital mess or another. I've definitely reached some conclusions about what makes a successful union.

Still, offering up my observations for public consumption is a tricky proposition. By their very nature they imply, perhaps wrongly, that I know what others don't. Yes, Renee and I have made it . . . so far. But assuming we live out normal life spans, we've got another thirty or thirty-five years to go. And I'm smart enough to know that anything can happen in that length of time.

Nevertheless, as one rushing in where angels fear to tread, I've compiled here a few of our "secrets," which really aren't secrets at all. They're common sense.

Consider these ingredients for marital happiness if you're thinking of getting hitched, or if you're already wed but things aren't working too well.

Luck. You can hook up with someone who seems perfectly fine all through your courtship, only to discover after the "I do's" that he or she is a closet drug addict, drunk, spouse beater, philanderer, child abuser, schizophrenic, or narcissist.

In choosing a spouse, hardly anything works better than just plain dumb luck.

Humor. One thing that has saved Renee and me is that we both like to laugh—with each other and at each other. We laugh about our parents. We laugh about sex. When we were poor we laughed about once having to exist on eggs for several days.

We also rarely miss an opportunity to good-naturedly insult each other. Some people misunderstand this.

One night, waiting in the lobby of a seafood restaurant, my son and I were standing near the lobster tank. Renee stood a few feet away. I pointed to one particularly hideous lobster.

"Hey," I said, "there's Mom."

Renee grinned. She pointed to a painting of a huge, spouting whale.

"Look, there's Dad," she said.

It was love, Prather-style. But I remember the astonished face of a stranger who overheard.

Tolerance. No two people were ever more different than Renee and I. She enjoys action: rowdy basketball games, church socials, vacations to crowded beaches—preferably with half of her enormous family along. I like leaning back in my recliner before a roaring fire with a thick book.

I used to try to change Renee. She used to try to change me. Finally we decided that neither of us was likely to change very much. We learned to appreciate and love each other for what we are. Occasionally I go to the beach with her; occasionally she sits by the fire with me. But mostly we allow each other to do what we really want to do.

Religion. We've found it helpful that we agree strongly on the basics of our religion. Faith provides us certain shared, core assumptions about our relationship—that our marriage is sacred and that God wants us to stay together, for example.

A strong belief in God doesn't guarantee anyone a blissful relationship.

Still, statistically, study after study has found that if both partners profess an abiding faith in the Almighty and attend church regularly, they're less likely to divorce and far more likely to report that they're genuinely happy with their spouses.

They even report having more satisfying sex than nonreligious couples. (Godliness, Saint Paul said, is profitable for all things!)

Besides, on the days we really despise each other, Renee and I find it comforting to pray together. Sometimes we pray for each other. Sometimes we pray against each other.

Servitude. This isn't a popular word anymore, but I think it's among the most important ones. Whenever I hear spouses ciphering up their rights—"I washed dishes five times last week and you only washed them twice!"—I figure they're in big trouble.

Renee and I have always felt we were here to serve each other. She's my helpmate. I'm hers. My job is to keep her happy. Her job is to keep me happy.

Neither of us cares much about equality or even fairness.

When our son was an infant and Renee wanted more time with him, I took an extra job so she wouldn't have to work so much at her bank. At another point, my workdays were more flexible than hers; I became our son's caregiver.

Come to our house unannounced and you might find her mowing the yard—or me doing laundry. When I'm spending long hours writing or preparing sermons, Renee does virtually all the housework. We don't keep score.

Forgiveness. Neither of us holds a grudge for more than a day or two; it's counterproductive. We know we're only human beings and that we're prone to err. We try to be slow to anger and quick to forgive. And we rarely remind each other of past wrongs.

Luck. Yeah, I know I said that. But, really, luck is so important it needs to be mentioned twice.

THIS WEEK'S MEDITATION:

"Grant me the insight to choose the mate whom You know will be best for me and for our children. If I've already chosen a partner who seems less than perfect—they all are less than perfect—please give us the love, patience, and maturity to work together toward solving our problems."

A COVENANT IS
WHY WE STAY

Renee and I were married during Thanksgiving weekend, 1978. We held our wedding in the country church where she had grown up and which her parents had helped start when they were the youngest couple in the congregation. By the time we married, her parents were among the church's older couples. Now Renee and I are middle-aged, and her parents are retired.

My father, who is a minister, performed our ceremony. Minutes before I stepped into the church's sanctuary to stand near the podium and wait for Renee to walk down the aisle, I huddled in a tiny antechamber with my dad, I in my rented tuxedo, he in his clerical robes. I could feel the sweat beading on my upper lip.

My dad appraised me, his only son, then swallowed wetly and said, "Well, I guess this is it, huh?"

I swallowed, too. Finally I whispered, "I guess so."

In that antechamber, alone with my father for the last time before leaving him and my mother to establish a separate family, I got smacked by the full impact of what I'd agreed to do. If I could have run, I might have. In that one sweaty moment, I re-

103

alized I was about to yoke myself with a woman for the rest of my life.

I was only twenty-two, and I was going to stand before God, our families, and our friends and swear to never again have another woman. Until then, I'd never managed to be faithful for more than a few months to any other girl I'd dated. Now I was vowing to give this one fifty years, maybe more. What if I changed my mind later? Or she changed hers?

Somehow, by the grace of God, I found the composure and courage to walk out of that room anyway, in the right direction. But I've never been more frightened.

In last week's meditation, I told you we've made it two decades now, a truth that constantly amazes me. I offered up some of our "secrets." But there's one key reason we've thrived together that I didn't mention last week. It's more complicated than the others, and I saved it so I'd have the space to elaborate on it a bit.

First let me tell you what it's not. The longer Renee and I are married, the less I believe that the cornerstone of a good marriage is love. Or at least not "love" as exemplified by the silliness you see on television, where two swells maintain a nonstop ardor despite their children, their bills, and their jobs. That's fantasy.

No, I think the true foundation is something else.

It's sheer stubbornness, a jaw-gritting determination to see it through.

When we stood up and took that oath in 1978, Renee and I both knew we'd entered a covenant with God. Cold as it may seem, this idea of a covenant is the blunt scriptural idea that underpins marriage and many other agreements.

You find covenants throughout the Bible. When God wanted to bind Himself eternally with Abraham's descendants, He made a covenant with Abraham and sealed it in blood. Once pledged, it could never be broken. When young David and his friend Jonathan swore to remain closer than brothers, they likewise made a covenant. As a result, even after Jonathan was killed in battle, David supported Jonathan's survivors for the rest of his life.

Typically a covenant is entered into with great emotion, but its power has little to do with feelings. It's a contract, plain and simple. The contract remains in force after the feelings wane.

Faith in God is a kind of covenant. I believe in God not because I always want to, but because I once promised Him I'd believe. There are days when having that faith is easy: I feel as if God is right beside me. Other days, I think God must be a black hole out in the universe somewhere or only a figment of my imagination.

Still, I go on believing. It's a question of my will, not my feelings. It's a matter of being a man of my word.

In the same way, Renee and I swore we'd be true to each other until we died. And we're going to do it—if it kills us. That doesn't sound romantic. But romance ebbs and flows over the years. Between those lovey-dovey spells, you discover new emotions toward your mate, including boredom, disappointment, and claustrophobia.

Yet if you see your marriage as a covenant, you're still obligated.

It can be rough. But there's also a hidden beauty to all this. When you know you're obligated to somebody for life, you tend to grow up. You make accommodations. You learn to compromise, forgive, adjust. Marriage then, in a sense, becomes a mutual wearing down—which paradoxically builds incredibly powerful bonds.

I'm constantly amazed by the wonder of it. The covenant Renee and I made, which we've kept with difficulty, has melded us together as one person. Renee already knows my secrets and honors them. She sees my faults and accepts them. Who wants to go through that taxing process again with somebody new? Not I.

I make few judgments about people whose marriages have ended, mind you. Understandably, many people get worn out with the vast accumulation of irritations. Others have to deal with partners who've gone stone crazy.

As fate would have it, though, Renee and I both are fairly normal. We're the usual mixture of virtues and faults, insights and ignorance. Fortunately, we don't have to contend with sheer insanity. And so far we haven't quit.

There still are days when I think Renee is the most wonderful woman on this planet. Other days, I feel she's not so wonderful. Whatever the case, I stay. So does she.

I call it stubbornness, the keeping of our covenant. But I suspect that stubbornness may be the central attribute of genuine—and lasting—love.

THIS WEEK'S MEDITATION:

"Lord, give me the wisdom to understand a marriage covenant, the love to enter one, and the strength to stay in it."

WE ALL NEED A
BACK PORCH TO ESCAPE
LIFE'S STORMS

Sometimes I practice back porch religion. That's the faith I join when life becomes too nerve-racking. I know I'm ready for my temporary conversion whenever my attitude starts reminding me of a guy I once worked for in a house-painting crew. Some mornings he would show up glowering as if he could bite the head off a tenpenny nail.

"Boys, don't mess with me today," he'd warn us. "I don't like nothin' nor nobody."

I can relate. Right now it's not any one problem that makes me want to pull out my hair (or somebody else's). It's the accumulation of a thousand small things.

Heck, just reading the news is stressful, much less writing and preaching about it. I daily monitor several news organizations and wire services on the Internet, looking for fodder for my sermons and the weekly column I still write for a half dozen newspapers.

If you think your local newspaper contains horror stories,

you ought to read the ones that don't make it into print. The Web daily carries hundreds of articles from around the globe about serial murders, scandals, mass rapes, genocide, fallen heroes.

Meanwhile I receive letters, e-mail, and phone messages that probably don't amount to much in the scheme of eternity, but some days seem to swirl around me like 747s stacked above a big-city airport—and my air control radar is on the blink.

Meanwhile, an elderly member of my church has suffered a heart attack and is languishing in the coronary care unit of a large hospital forty miles away. His son has called to ask if I can hurry to his bedside. I'll go, but it means sacrificing my day off.

Another man who quit my church in a snit over some unknown triviality—without attempting to reconcile or even bothering to say good-bye—has fallen on hard times. A parishioner wants me to take up a special offering for him on Sunday. I know I should do it. It would be the charitable thing. But I don't feel very charitable.

Recently, when I was in a more generous mood, I helped my congregation sell a piece of property we owned to another church. At my suggestion, we sold the land for substantially less than it was worth, as a favor to this other group, trying to help them. We already were doing rather well financially for a small congregation such as ours, and to me helping these fellow Christians seemed like an appropriate gesture of gratitude to God. Now someone in the congregation we helped is telling people around town that we overcharged them, that I had some ulterior motive in coming to their aid.

As I said, I'm not feeling nearly so benevolent today.

The yard needs mowing but the mower blade is dull. The automatic garage door opener has started raising and lowering the door of its own volition. The car is leaking oil. The heating element on our dryer broke yesterday and the repairman is late; wet clothes hang everywhere.

Your life, I imagine, is as hectic as mine.

If you're a teacher, you cope with petty colleagues waging departmental turf battles, not to mention all the dim-witted students whose crosses you bear. If you're a doctor, a patient is suing you. If you're unemployed, the bank wants to repossess your motorcycle. Your religious denomination is splintering. It's been raining for weeks, and terrorists are threatening to blow up the eastern seaboard pretty soon. The stock market's teetering.

There are times when I simply can't take any more. You likely feel the same.

These are the times I fulfill the few duties I absolutely can't avoid—and then retreat to the seclusion of the wooden deck behind my house, my private chapel. It's hidden to the left by high shrubs and to the right by a corner of the house and a long grassy slope. The rear of the yard is lined with pine trees and adjoins an empty field. I leave the cordless phone inside the house. I leave the cellular in my car. I can sit on that deck and escape everyone on earth except my wife and son, whose company I usually enjoy. I can watch rabbits romp and blue jays play tag.

I'll rearrange my whole schedule, postpone meetings, and relax out there half the day, alone in the sun, reading a mystery novel. If I crack the Bible at all, I skim past Lamentations and Revelation and the other gloom and hellfire books. I thumb to Psalms or the gospels, books of hope. The Psalmist reminds me that the Lord wants me to lie down in green pastures and rest beside still waters. On warm, dry evenings, Renee and I lie on that deck on a quilt, picking out figures in the clouds and telling jokes.

Occasionally, everyone must escape the harshness of the real world.

For a while, we need to see only the people we want to see and think only the thoughts we want to think. Or perhaps see no one and think nothing.

THIS WEEK'S MEDITATION:

"I need a refuge, a secret place to hide when the world becomes too much to bear. Please help me find such a place, no matter how humble—my porch, a shady corner of the local park, an isolated pew in the balcony of my church, a nook in the attic. I need a spot where I can be alone with You, and with myself. I need the time and courage to go there."

Week

CHEERFUL GIVERS

"Give and it will be given to you; a good measure, pressed down,
shaken together and running over will be put into your lap by men."

LUKE 6:38

God loves cheerful givers, the Bible says, and He blesses such folks with spiritual gifts and even with financial abundance. I've frequently heard preachers express the principle like this: "You can't outgive God."

But giving freely is a hard discipline to develop, particularly if we don't have an abundance ourselves. There's something innate in most of us, call it an instinct toward self-preservation or the sin of selfishness, or both, that demands we look out for ourselves before we worry about anyone else.

If I understand the Scripture correctly on this point, it calls us to override this quite logical instinct. It demands that we grow as humans, that we learn to see beyond our own wants and needs. But placing the good of others above our own good requires self-discipline and love. It also requires faith, a hearty belief in an unseen God who notices our secret generosity and is both willing and able to reward it.

Once, for the Sunday night service at the rural church of which I then was the pastor, I'd invited in a guest speaker, a lay minister who also runs a successful business in our county seat.

I'd asked the treasurer to cut a thirty-five-dollar check for the speaker, to reimburse him—feebly—for his time. But as the service started, I suddenly decided to take up an offering for him, too. Don't ask me why.

I assumed we'd take up an additional twenty dollars if we were lucky. There were only about thirty people present, mostly elderly folks subsisting on Social Security and working-class couples barely scraping by on factory or body-shop wages, and we'd taken our usual weekly offerings that morning. Back then, we never took collections on Sunday nights. Nevertheless, we passed the plate.

Then the guest speaker stepped to the podium. I'd asked him to tell the story of his conversion from his former life as a drug addict to his current one as a clean and sober Christian, and he did.

But then he veered off onto the subject of giving. He said that when he initially was converted, he was unemployed and living on food stamps. He decided to trust the Almighty to provide for his needs—and the Spirit seemed to impress on him that he must first become a giver to others before God would give to him.

He told stories illustrating that God had many times returned his own charity to him. Once, he said, he'd dropped his last fifty dollars in the collection plate at church. It was the only money he had to buy heating fuel for the week. On his way home, his nonchurchgoing brother flagged him down in the middle of the road and paid off a hundred-dollar debt the brother had owed him for years.

When the service ended, I reminded the speaker not to leave until I could get his honorarium check from the treasurer and we could count the offering we'd taken for him.

"I don't want it," he said. "Give the money to somebody here who has a need."

"Are you sure?" I asked.

"Yeah. Give it to somebody in your church."

I thanked him and he left. Several members of our congregation continued to mill around the sanctuary chatting in groups of two or three, as rural parishioners always do.

Most, I knew, were struggling financially. Normally, I would have had to think about who needed the money worst. Normally, I would have talked it over with the treasurer or my wife. But as soon as the guest speaker said what he did, clearly an image popped into my mind: a young woman named Stacy.

I'd seen my wife helping the treasurer count the offering. She walked up.

"How much was in the plate?" I said.

"A lot," she said. "At least seventy-five dollars, maybe more."

Actually, when I checked with the treasurer, it turned out to be eighty-five dollars. I took the money and also asked the treasurer to make out that thirty-five-dollar check—to Stacy. All told, we now had $120 for her.

I caught the young woman's eye and motioned for her to come over. I told her quietly what had happened and handed her the money. She burst into tears. I knew she'd been having a hard time. Her husband was out of work. She held a modest job as a receptionist. They were hard-pressed to pay their bills. Even so, her reaction seemed out of proportion to the size of the gift.

Here's what I didn't know. When she'd recovered enough to talk, Stacy told me her story. Late that very afternoon, she'd visited a friend. As she prepared to leave this other woman's house, Stacy had felt compelled to give her twenty dollars. She hadn't understood why. She couldn't spare it. She argued against the urge, but couldn't shake it. Finally, she'd secretly written a twenty-dollar check and hidden it in a basket in her friend's bathroom, where the woman wouldn't find it until Stacy was gone.

Then Stacy came directly to church—and unexpectedly received back six times what she'd just given. That's why she'd sobbed. She was certain she knew where the donation came from. It wasn't from our speaker or me.

I mulled that over myself. Stacy gave, even though she was needy. Then something moved me to take up a rare Sunday night offering. Something moved the congregation to donate freely. Something moved the guest speaker to refuse what was rightfully his. Something moved me to give the money to Stacy.

Maybe it was all a big circular coincidence.

But I never told Stacy that. It wouldn't have done any good. She was too certain that you couldn't outgive God.

THIS WEEK'S MEDITATION:

"Let me see beyond my own wants to those of my friends, my family, and total strangers. As I learn to help others, I ask You, Lord, to repay me from Your secret storehouse."

TAKE HEART, YOU LOSERS

For years I've enjoyed reading the Bible more than any other book. It's just so relevant, as current as today's TV news broadcast or church business meeting.

I've come to think that mainly it's a book about people who were religious failures, or who at the very least were people of mixed morals—and about a God who loved them anyway.

Most of the Bible's heroes did accomplish noble deeds, but with the exception of Jesus they also descended at times into violence, thievery, egotism, adultery, or another of the countless human frailties. In that regard their names are almost interchangeable with those of Jimmy Swaggart or Jim Bakker or Bill Clinton or the hapless sinner destined to hit the headlines next.

Take, for example, Abraham, the great patriarch of Genesis. His spiritual and physical descendants make up half our world's population: Christians, Jews, and Muslims all claim him as their father. He was renowned as God's personal friend.

On the other hand, the Scriptures also tell us that Abraham disobeyed God by conceiving a son, Ishmael, with his wife's maid. When that caused tensions at home, Abraham abandoned Ishmael and his mother to the desert, where they might have died of exposure had God not intervened. Elsewhere in his journeys, fearing for his life, Abraham twice claimed that his wife, Sarah, was merely his sister—and offered her as a sexual gift to foreign kings.

Then there was Rahab, an ancestor of Jesus, who earned her bread as a lady of the evening. Samson killed thirty men to pay off a wager. He also consorted with prostitutes over a period of decades, dangerous liaisons that ultimately cost him his job, freedom, and life. Today we'd say he suffered from a sexual addiction.

King David sent one of his soldiers, Uriah, to his death in an attempt to cover up David's affair with Uriah's wife, Bathsheba. David also proved to be the world's worst dad: One of his sons raped his own sister, Tamar; another son, Absalom, killed his rapist brother to avenge their sister and then was himself executed while leading a revolution against David. The king's surviving son, Solomon, became the wisest man on earth, but eventually started worshiping pagan gods; his son, David's grandson, lost the family's kingdom. The mighty prophet Elisha was sensitive about his baldness. He got so mad when a crowd of boys jeered at his shiny dome that he sicced bears on them. Forty-two were torn to shreds.

The New Testament's stars don't fare much better. Peter denied Christ to save his own skin. Later, after he had become the head of the early church, he taught false doctrine in an attempt to remain popular with Christians of Jewish ancestry. Young John Mark chickened out on a missionary journey and abandoned Paul and his coworker, Barnabas. When John Mark asked for a second chance to accompany the dynamic duo, Paul and Barnabas disagreed so strongly over whether he should be allowed to go that they dissolved their partnership.

Were all these people simply bums?

No. Certainly they had their regrettable days, as we all do. But mainly these people also were sincere servants of God, men and women who prayed to do good and suffered wretchedly when they fell short. They couldn't help failing sooner or later; they were human.

The writers of Scripture generally didn't seem to have a problem with recording such human complexities and contradictions. And even we moderns can tolerate sinful leaders when they're confined to the dusty pages of the Bible.

It's in the here-and-now that we have trouble dealing with them. When one of our deacons pilfers cash from the church building fund, we cry for his head to be served us on a platter. When a TV minister is revealed to be living in splendor while begging his viewers for donations, we twist our faces and cry, "I knew there was nothing to him!"

Well, maybe there's something good within such fellows anyhow.

Let's get this much straight: If you regularly attend a church or a temple, or vote in elections, or work in an office, sooner or later your leaders will disappoint you, perhaps dreadfully so. That's not because religion—or even politics or business—is made up of worse people than you find elsewhere in society. It's because they're populated by the very same people you find elsewhere. Even in the church, anointed servants of God occasionally commit ugly deeds. Truth is, wherever He's at work, God employs flawed people to fulfill His purposes. They're the only kind available.

If you take it as a whole, that's what the Bible is about: wretched people trying to do good but often failing, and a God who forgives them when no one else will.

One wise woman explained this principle to King David during the worst of his domestic disasters: "For we must all surely die, and are as water spilled on the ground, which cannot be gathered up again," she said. "Yet God does not take away life, but instead devises ways to keep the banished person from being expelled from Him."

THIS WEEK'S MEDITATION:

*"I will strive to be less dismissive of others when I see their faults.
I will remember that under God's eyes we all are laid bare.
But as God has chosen to overlook my sins, I will overlook others'.
I will do this not to deny the myriad and long-lasting consequences
of their wrongdoing, but to show godly compassion."*

KENTUCKY'S "KING" SOLOMON

Among the more remarkable stories I know is the tale of William "King" Solomon, a real-life figure who lived through the cholera pandemic that ravaged Europe and America in the 1830s.

In 1891, long after Solomon's death, a popular author of that day, James Lane Allen, included a moving short story about him in Allen's book *Flute and Violin and Other Kentucky Tales and Romances*. Currently *The Kentucky Encyclopedia* includes an entry on Solomon, and David Dick, a former CBS News correspondent, recently featured him as a character in Dick's acclaimed historical novel *The Scourges of Heaven*.

Admittedly, in reading about Solomon I find it difficult to parse the facts from the legend. But the bulk of the tale is true.

If Solomon were here he'd probably be amazed that people still are talking about him. A native of Virginia, he moved to Lexington, Kentucky, as a young fellow in the 1790s. A tall, muscular specimen, he earned his keep by digging cellars.

Sadly, he also displayed a passion for the liquor jug. By the early 1830s, when Solomon would have been in his fifties, he had become the town drunk. Unable or unwilling to work, homeless, he wandered Lexington in rags and slept in doorways.

Lexington then was a center of culture, education, and aristocracy frequently referred to as "The Athens of the West." It also was the hometown of Henry Clay, who still ranks among history's great statesmen.

The locals were embarrassed by Solomon's presence. For sport, certain wags took to calling the hapless drunkard "King" Solomon. In June 1833, a Lexington court declared him a vagrant with no means of support. Near the courthouse, the sheriff publicly auctioned Solomon as an indentured servant. The highest bidder would own his services as a laborer for a year. A crowd jeered him as he stood at the auction block.

In Allen's partly fictionalized telling of the story, a law student shouted that the rag picker should buy Solomon to get his clothes. A medical student bid $1.50, remarking that the old drunk would likely die within the year—and the student could use his body to practice dissecting.

As the bids escalated, an elderly, free black woman named Aunt Charlotte pushed her way through the crowd. To the crowd's astonishment, she began bidding, too, and, in Allen's story, won Solomon's services for the sum of $13.

That much, at least, is fact: Solomon, a white man, was bought by Aunt Charlotte, a former slave who had known him many years before when she was a slave governess in Virginia and Solomon was the playmate of her master's son. This must only have deepened his shame, if he had any shame left.

Aunt Charlotte apparently purchased Solomon because she couldn't bear to see him sold into bondage. When the crowd drifted away, she quickly set him free. Allen says she even offered Solomon the use of a spare room in her house, which he accepted.

The day after the auction, cholera erupted in Lexington. People began dying gruesomely, by the dozens. Nearly everyone in the city panicked. They packed wagons to flee to the country, desperate to escape the disease. Some abandoned their sick relatives.

Among those who departed were the city's grave diggers.

Aunt Charlotte and King Solomon were preparing to flee as well when they learned that bodies were piling up at the cemetery because no one remained to bury them. Solomon gathered up a set of cellar-digging tools, walked to the cemetery, and started hollowing out a grave. When he'd finished that grave, Solomon dug another. Apparently no one had thought to ask for his help. He just gave it. Aunt Charlotte stayed in town to look after him.

All that summer, at the risk of his life, he dug grave after grave. Often he worked through the night. Exhausted, he'd collapse in a half-finished hole, sleep a few hours, and then continue his labors.

Frequently, he was the only living person present for these stark funerals. Some of those he buried were the men—or families of the men—who earlier had ridiculed him.

Eventually the cholera subsided. Survivors returned to Lexington. Society returned to normal, more or less. Solomon returned to his jug.

That fall, the courts opened. On the first day, it was rumored that the mighty Clay might argue a case, an event that always drew a packed house.

As Allen tells it, King Solomon was among those who pressed into the courtroom. He took an obscure seat in a corner against a wall.

The courtroom fell silent as the judge entered and sat at the bench. For a moment he studied the crowd—and spied Solomon. Alone one night during the plague, Solomon had buried the judge's wife and daughter.

The spectators waited for the justice to start the session's business.

Instead, spontaneously, he rose, straightened his robe, stepped into the crowd.

All eyes followed him. He walked back to Solomon, stood before him.

Then, solemnly, the judge shook the old drunk's hand. The judge tried to speak, but was too overcome by emotion. He turned and walked toward the bench.

As he walked away, an elite member of the bar stood. Like the judge, he strode to the back of the courtroom. He, too, shook Solomon's hand. In turn, each lawyer in the room also stood and came to grasp the grave digger's callused paw. The spectators lined up to follow the lawyers. Men from every stratum of society filed by.

Solomon at first appeared confused. Then, as he recognized they were honoring him, he started to weep. Soon everyone in the courtroom was crying.

Here's how Allen concludes his version nearly sixty years later:

"Such power has a single act of mortal greatness to reverse the relations of men, lifting up one, and bringing all others to do him homage.

"It was the coronation scene in the life of old King Solomon of Kentucky."

William Solomon died in the poorhouse in 1854. Citizens of Lexington bought his coffin and laid him to rest in splendorous Lexington Cemetery. In 1908 they erected a prominent monument to him there. You can see it today. In tourist appeal it perhaps ranks second only to Henry Clay's massive sepulchre. The inscription near "King" Solomon's name reads: "For Had He Not a Royal Heart."

Solomon's tomb continues to bear witness to a spark of potential nobility that resides within the heart of every human, no matter how humble his or her station.

THIS WEEK'S MEDITATION:

"Lord, let me appreciate the nobility of all who surround me—the busboy, the waitress, the factory worker, the mechanic, the grave digger, my children, the homeless person, the welfare mother."

ON SOFTBALL, AGE, AND ACCEPTANCE

I planted my spikes in the damp sand of the batter's box and squinted toward the other team's outfielders bouncing on their heels beneath the ballpark's lights. It was the bottom of the final inning. My church's slow-pitch softball team already had one out. We were narrowly trailing our opponents in a tough, close game.

But we also had runners on two bases. Our team's fate rested largely on me.

Immediately I saw the opening I wanted. The other squad's left-center fielder had drifted too far to my left. The right-center fielder stood too far to the right. Directly over second base lay a lane wide enough to pave a four-lane highway on.

All I had to do was crack a solid line drive over the pitcher's head and drop the ball in the dewy grass. It would bounce to the fence before the outfielders could reach it.

By that time, our two swift runners would have scored. I'd be safely on first base, maybe on second. The game would be ours.

My teammates shouted encouragement. My wife and sisters-in-law, sitting behind our dugout on aluminum bleachers, cheered, too. "Woo, go honey!" my wife yelled.

The pitcher nervously began his brief windup and released the ball. For a moment it seemed to hang, suspended at the top of its arc on the evening breeze.

Then the ball dropped, slow and fat, across the center of the plate. Perfect. I lifted my left foot and stepped into my swing and felt the ping of the aluminum bat.

Instantly I knew. In my eagerness to run I had leaned toward first base before I'd actually met the ball, and as a result I'd merely clipped the ball off the bottom of my bat.

The ball didn't shoot over the pitcher's head. It trickled directly to him on the ground. He lurched forward, scooped it up, and fired it to the second baseman.

One runner out.

I lumbered down the baseline. The throw to first beat me by at least five steps.

Double play. Game over.

Like a portly Charlie Brown, I wasn't the hero I'd anticipated. I was the goat. Not that my teammates—or my wife—said so. The men of our church are a nice bunch and we'd all agreed from the season's start that we wouldn't take the games too seriously. Plus, I'm their pastor. No one really wants to bawl out the preacher over a softball gaffe.

But for a while I couldn't help chewing out myself.

You see, I played summer softball years ago, too, back in my youth and glory.

My very first season, I was on a team that won our league's championship. At that season's end, I was named to the league's all-star squad, specifically for my batting.

Back then, I could hit the ball wherever I wanted it to go—to any spot where the opposing team didn't have a defensive player standing ready.

Twenty-five years later, I can't place the ball on the playing field any more than I can place the planets in the solar system. I'm slower, fatter. I step to the plate with far less self-assurance. That's middle age. By the time you reach it, you've hit bloopers on so many of life's playing fields, you've faced your own limitations for so long, that you're no longer certain what will happen when you smack a softball or, for that matter, when you sit down to write a book or research a sermon.

So I moped for a day or two. I didn't allow myself to stay depressed. It's not wise to worry about what you can't control.

Soon I forced myself to think of it all in another way. In life, everything's a trade-off. Physically I'm not the kid I used to be. But today I know a lot of important things I didn't a quarter century ago. I can, for example, view my softball errors in a larger context, a comforting one.

At forty-two, I can truly appreciate now the value of a breezy summer night and a brightly lit ballpark and the happy chatter of women in the stands. As a youth I took such treasures for granted, as rights to which I was entitled by my own strength. Now I know they're privileges I've been temporarily loaned and which will be recalled soon enough.

Today I cherish far more than I once did the friendship of a team of good-hearted guys. I know how transitory such brotherhood can be.

I recognize the gift of the game itself, no matter how poorly played. When I stepped up to the plate that night, intent on hitting a line drive that never happened, I was, at least, absorbed in the sanctity of that pure, physical act. I had no idea what the state of the economy might be or whether I was popular at my job. For a few seconds, the universe consisted of me and the pitch and the possibilities.

Today I know to savor such moments, even when my team loses. Even when I've caused it to lose. Some forms of grace are manifested to us only through age and loss.

THIS WEEK'S MEDITATION:

"I thank you, God, for the sheer joy of a damp summer night in a community ballpark. I thank you for the smell of mown grass and the sound of a cheering woman who loves me. I thank you for arms with which to swing a bat, even when I swing it badly. Help me remember that these are the true gifts—and that scores and batting averages are, by comparison, inconsequential."

WHAT MY MOTHER'S INNER PEACE TAUGHT ME

When I was a child my mom, Alice Prather, was like one of those TV sitcom mothers of the 1950s and 1960s. She was a full-time homemaker whose life seemed to revolve around my dad, my sister, and me.

It was a different time. Mom cooked three meals a day, baked cookies, washed clothes, refereed fights, mended stubbed toes. My dad earned our keep as a preacher and schoolteacher, a feat still possible then.

Later, when I was in high school, financial hardship forced my mother to go to work outside the home, as a teacher's aide and later as a school secretary. She ended up working in the public schools for twenty years. She obviously liked that a lot, too. She built a network of new friends.

Yet when I was a kid I assumed that Mom loved doing the things she did for us, that there was nowhere she'd rather be than at home with my sister, Cathi, and me. I continue to believe that ultimately she was glad to be there.

I think that what I admire about her most is her unusual ability to adapt—to her era, to her expected role, to her financial circumstances—while remaining at peace within herself even as those times, roles, and circumstances have changed. It's a talent that not many people possess and that our society tends not to value.

She's not a true stoic. She does express emotions, including joy and grief and, from time to time, irritability. But she's never been a complainer, a malcontent. I've never heard her raise her voice in anger. She's always tended to perform any task put before her with a self-contained patience, whether it was mopping up my sister's spilled orange juice or typing a letter for a school administrator. Somehow she seemed at ease in almost any role.

I realize now that her earlier years with us as a full-time mother could be tedious, that they required sacrifices, and that often Mom's duties were frustrating. Once—after Cathi and I had followed her around the house for hours asking, "Mama, can I go outside to play?" and "Mama, can I have some pop?"— she turned on us and said, "Can't you all say anything besides 'Mama'? Call me 'Alice'!"

So we did. We started calling her Alice, her Christian name, which we later shortened to "Al." That's all we've called her for the last thirty years. It isn't what she had in mind. She was looking only for a temporary respite; we permanently renamed her. That would have aggravated some mothers. But Al responded with good humor.

I can imagine someone reading this and concluding that my mother has a problem, that she's unwilling to assert herself, that she's a hapless doormat.

That's not the case at all. She just has a different take on life.

Al grew up on a hardscrabble farm during the Depression. As an adult she's weathered surgeries and survived the loss of a full-term, healthy infant who died in childbirth because of a doctor's error.

As a result, she doesn't sweat the small things. She's got a sense of perspective. Call her Mom or call her Al or call her Roscoe. It's no big deal to her. She's endured a lot worse than that.

My sister's first marriage split up at about the time Al was entering late middle age. Cathi and her young son, Will, moved back into the house with my parents for roughly a decade. They all lived together in a small doublewide trailer. Cathi worked and returned to school, so my parents often were left helping raise her energetic son. It wasn't an easy situation. Cathi frequently fell into depression. My dad occasionally chafed at this interruption of what he'd hoped would be his quiet later years.

Al just smiled and cooked Will's food and helped him with his homework and washed his clothes and drove him to baseball practice, and then walked around humming to herself. I've tried to adopt her worldview as my own: Roll with the punches.

From my mom I've also learned the talent of listening. My dad, my sister, and I are all talkers—opinionated, brash. Al is by nature quiet. When I was young, she always had time to hear me prattle on and on about my day at school. She rarely made critical judgments or offered unsought advice. She listened, and that was enough.

In addition to that, she gave me a sense of humor. My father is the public entertainer, a preacher and storyteller. But my mom's the wit, although few outside our family know it. With one well-placed comment or a timely twist of her face, she can lay me out on the floor laughing.

The writer of Proverbs described another marvelous woman like this:

"Strength and dignity are her clothing, and she laughs at the time to come. She opens her mouth with wisdom, and the law of kindness is on her tongue. . . . Her children rise up and call her blessed."

I feel honored to have Al as my mom. I do think of her as a blessing.

For good or ill, our culture places a lot of weight on worldly achievement: political power, wealth, accolades from an adoring public. My mom has proven to me that in many ways the most valuable people can also be the quietest.

THIS WEEK'S MEDITATION:

"God, You said, 'Honor your father and mother.' Help me show respect to those who gave me life, and who not only loved me first, but have loved me longest."

WE'RE SHAPED BY PREDESTINATION AND FREE WILL

A half dozen framed photographs of our son, John, taken at various stages of his childhood, hang on a wall at the top of our house's only staircase. In a bedroom we keep two photo albums that are stuffed with pictures of him. Such are the treasures collected by the parents of only children.

In each of his early childhood pictures, John looks so much like his mother did at the same ages that it's eerie. He was blond as a youngster, bony, freckled, handsome. Except for my wife's dresses and the length of her hair, she in her childhood pictures is nearly indistinguishable from my son in his.

Today, as a teenager, though, John bears little real resemblance to those photographs of himself or to Renee. And he never has looked at all like me, then or now. I was stocky as a youth, a lineman on football teams. Even at fifteen, John easily could hide behind a highway mile marker.

Once, when he was small, I took him and my wife's nephew to a store. We ran into a friend of mine I hadn't seen for years.

"These guys are my son and my nephew," I announced.

"Hey, I knew your dad a long, long time ago," my friend said—to my wife's nephew.

As much as John doesn't resemble me physically, he does resemble me in other ways. When he was about seven, an adult asked him who he took after most, his dad or his mom. "Well, I look like my mom," he said, "but I act like my dad."

To a large degree, that's true.

My own father always has claimed that the first word I spoke was "Why?" Now I know what he meant. As soon as he learned to talk, John began chattering constantly, and didn't stop until he passed through puberty. He asked questions about everything.

Like me, he loved TV and movies—and still does—but it was infuriating back then, trying to watch a show with him if you cared about hearing the actor's lines: "Hey, Dad, why isn't that guy wearing a bulletproof vest?" he'd ask. "Did the police have bulletproof vests when you were a kid? Have you ever seen one?"

As a teenager he's grown progressively more introverted. I went through an identical stage. Ironically, now it irritates him if I try to talk to him during his favorite sitcoms. But we like the same shows. He rarely misses *Saturday Night Live*, which was one of my favorites in the 1970s. And we listen to the same music. He sits around the house for hours at a stretch picking Lynyrd Skynyrd and Led Zeppelin songs on his guitar. I listened to those bands. John loves to play jokes on his mom; so do I.

There are many other things about my son that are unlike either my wife or me.

He seems far more concerned with—but shyer toward—the opposite sex than either of us was at his age.

Neither Renee nor I, as adults anyway, has much patience with pets. Our son would adopt anything that draws breath: cats, dogs, ponies. A fat, sleepy feline follows him everywhere. He strokes it, talks to it. I hate cats.

John's more spiritual than Renee and I were as kids. Neither of us gave a hoot about God back then. John plays drums in our church's worship band. I frequently find him reading his Bible when I pass by his room late at night. He's active in our congregation's youth group.

What does this all mean?

Well, some Southern Baptists have begun again to debate predestination, the old doctrine that says God preordained some of us for eternal salvation and others for damnation. Psychologists and geneticists still argue over how much of our personality is biologically predetermined and how much is the result of our upbringing. Others rail about whether our intelligence is racially ordained or whether it's a matter of schooling.

All these are fascinating, worthy issues. But I doubt they'll ever be answered. Our lives in this world—and even our eternal destinies—are decided by strange confluences that none of us can ever fully understand, minglings of neurons, hormones, DNA, and personal choices too complex to decipher.

We're born with much of our destiny already decided for us: our skin color, our height, the shape of our bodies, and much of our intelligence. We don't choose our parents, and heaven knows they play a role in determining matters ranging from our ability to form lasting relationships to whether we'll believe in God. But still other things we choose for ourselves: whether to heed wise counsel, whether we'll work hard or hardly work.

We're shaped by divine will and by free will. We're driven by the gods our mothers worshiped and by the patent medicines our great-grandfathers drank and by the theories our second-grade teachers learned in continuing education seminars.

Parenthood proves at least this much to me. In the final estimation, we're all mysteries, every last one of us.

THIS WEEK'S MEDITATION:

"Lord, we are, as the Psalmist said many years ago, 'Fearfully and wonderfully made.' Help us to recognize and honor the holy mystery that each human being represents. Help us especially to see that divine wonder in the lives of our own children."

Saint Paul said that if we were wise, we would learn to imitate Jesus in our daily lives. I used to think that was a daunting request, and in some ways I still think so.

After all, I believe Jesus was and is the Son of God. I believe that when He walked on the earth He was sinless. That pretty much lets me out right there.

But the longer I muse on the Scriptures, the more I think I understand at least part of what Saint Paul was getting at. There are many attributes Jesus possessed that we actually can put into practice, whether in church or in our families or in the workplace.

Once I saw a book with the unlikely title of *Jesus CEO*. CEO, of course, stands for "chief executive officer." Apparently the author had decided to use Christ as a model for modern business leaders. I didn't give the book much thought at the time, and didn't buy it. But I've remained intrigued by that title.

As one who has worked in large corporations, I've come to think that had Jesus chosen to go into business, He actually could have been a wonderful corporate officer. True, He wasn't much concerned about declaring quarterly profits for shareholders.

But He certainly ought to be considered the most effective leader in history. He founded what has become the world's largest organization, the Christian faith, even though He began with little formal education, no money, and only twelve followers. Christianity with all its denominational subsidiaries has lasted two thousand years and is still growing. Two millennia later, people still revere Jesus. How many leaders can you say that about?

With that in mind I decided to restudy the four biblical gospels—Matthew, Mark, Luke, and John—in the hope of gleaning for myself some of Jesus' leadership principles. I've included scriptural references, so that you can look up passages that will, I hope, illustrate these points. Here's what I found about Jesus as a leader:

- He knew His own mission, trained for it single-mindedly, and never veered from it. See, for example, Luke 4:17-21.

- Jesus proved Himself loyal and obedient to His Boss. Jesus knew how to work under someone else's authority. See Luke 4:5-8 and John 12:48-50.

- Jesus aggressively challenged His competitor, Satan. See Luke 11:17-23.

- Jesus went where His customers were, from town to town, in the streets and in the temple. He didn't wait for the customers to come to Him. See John 7:1-29.

- He served His employees as much as He expected them to serve Him. See Luke 22:24-27 and John 13:3-17.

- He wasn't afraid to get close to His employees. Even though He possessed great power, He considered them His coworkers—and His personal friends. See John 15:14-17.

- He spoke boldly, and largely positively, to everyone. See Matthew 21:21-22.

- Jesus challenged common folks to view themselves as miracle workers. He not only assumed He could feed five thousand people with five loaves and two fish, He assumed His disciples could, too. "You give them something to eat," He said. See Luke 9:12-17.

- Jesus trained His workers by words and example. He always stated the rules clearly and succinctly. See Luke 6:20-44, Luke 10:1-16, and Luke 11:1-13.

- He insisted that His disciples remain in unity with each other. He knew well that a house divided will collapse. See Luke 11:17 and John 17:22-23.

- He was quick to correct errors among His workers before they got out of hand. See Mark 16:14.

- He protected His workers from outside raiders. See John 10:10-14.

- He constantly looked toward the future. He was a vision caster. He foresaw good times and bad, and prepared His followers for both. See John 16:16-33.

- He forgave others' errors and even resurrected the dead. See John 8:1-11 and John 11:1-46. (Similarly, wise leaders today give people second, third, and fourth chances. Sometimes they even bring back from the grave those whose careers might appear buried.)

- Jesus was Himself resurrected from the dead. When it looked as if He'd failed miserably, He made the ultimate comeback. He never quit. See John 20:19-31.

- Finally, Jesus knew when to step aside. See John 16:7. While He was still young, and at the moment of His greatest triumph, He turned over His organization to handpicked successors, got out of their way, and let them run it. Surely He saw that they weren't half as competent as He was, that they would stumble. But He knew the disciples could never progress to the next level, would never become mature leaders themselves, if He stayed and did all the work for them. "It's to your advantage that I go away," He said.

I've seen countless endeavors—from churches to corporations to families—fail because their leaders refused to hand over the mantle when it was time. If you wait until your successors are as qualified as you, you'll never relinquish control. After all, you've got ten or twenty more years of experience. But Jesus understood that for His disciples to grow, He had to go. He loved them—and the organization He'd started—more than He loved His earthly control over them. He loved them more than He craved their daily dependence upon Him for food and instructions.

He loved them enough to leave them.

THIS WEEK'S MEDITATION:

"In those arenas in which I exercise authority over others—
whether in the family, the office, or a house of worship—
I will endeavor to act as a creative and wise servant.
Help me become a leader whom others follow because of love."

JESUS WOULD HAVE
MADE YOU MAD

Last week we considered at Jesus as a leader, focusing mainly on
His more pleasing attributes, such as His generosity, vision, and
humility. But Jesus was many-layered, as are most great people,
and most nongreat people.

That's why I love Him. Not in the bumper-sticker sense of
"Honk If You Love Jesus." I love the Jesus we find as a literary
character in the New Testament gospels: the loving, acid-tongued,
spiritual, cranky rabbi who forgives prostitutes one minute and
scorches the epidermis off Pharisees and recalcitrant disciples
the next. He might have made a good business executive, but He
would've been a lousy politician.

My own reading of Jesus is that liberals and conservatives
alike would be about equally horrified if He showed up at their
next fund-raiser. Or at their churches. He wasn't, let's say, politically correct—whatever your politics. He wasn't even socially
correct. Here are a few more fun facts about Jesus:

· He and His disciples didn't wash their hands before
  they ate dinner. See Mark 7:1-8.

143

- He attended religious services, but wasn't welcome there because of His outspoken statements—such as the time He announced, unasked, that He was God's most anointed preacher. See Luke 4:16-30.

- Frequently He broke the Sabbath. See Matthew 12:1-14.

- He was ethnocentric. A Jew, He chose only other Jews as his chief disciples, socialized only with Jews, ministered almost exclusively to Jews. Once, a non-Jewish woman asked Him for help. Jesus called her a "dog." She won Him over by replying that even dogs get a share of the table scraps. See Matthew 15:21-28.

- Within Judaism, though, He was amazingly egalitarian. He enjoyed the company of tax collectors who sucked up to Roman occupation officials, fishermen, patriotic zealots, and hookers. See, for one example, Luke 19:2-10.

- He liked poor people better than rich people. He said most rich people would be barred from heaven. Luke 18:24-25.

- He loathed self-important religious leaders and merchants who used the temple for selling wares. He didn't mind taking the law into His own hands by physically throwing out peddlers who profited from religious items. See Mark 11:15-17.

- He demanded that His followers sell everything they owned and give the proceeds away. He once praised an impoverished, elderly widow for donating her last two pennies to the temple. (Imagine what the contemporary media would have made of that—Jesus, the original televangelist?) See Mark 12:41-44.

- He criticized those who prayed in public or sought acclaim when they gave money to charity. (Makes you wonder what His positions would have been on prayer at school graduations or on naming new wings at churches after wealthy benefactors.) See Matthew 6:1-6.

- He lived under a brutal, occupation government, but said nothing against it. He told people to pay their taxes even if the levies were unfair. See Matthew 22:15-21.

- For His closest friends He chose only men—twelve of them, all from the same geographical, religious, and ethnic heritage. See Matthew 10:1-4.

- He asked a woman He'd just met to fetch Him a drink. See John 4:4-27.

- He lived partly off the largess of several rich women. See Luke 8:1-3.

- He was a faith healer who frequently laid hands on the sick. Sometimes he worked cures by such unusual methods as spitting on people. See Mark 8:22-26.

- He thought mental illnesses were caused by demonic possession. He cast out such devils in dramatic exorcisms. See Matthew 17:14-18.

- He thought the Hebrew Bible was divinely inspired and absolutely accurate down to the last "jot" and "tittle." See Matthew 5:17-19.

- He preached a lot about hell and frequently told people they were likely to go there if they didn't obey what He told them. See Matthew 23:13-33 and Luke 10:13-15.

- Apparently He wasn't much concerned about family values. He never married or fathered children. He didn't get along well with His siblings or His more distant relatives, some of whom thought He was crazy. He even said publicly that His friends were as close to Him emotionally, and maybe closer, than His own mother.

    He sternly warned that the only way to become His disciple was to love Him more than you loved your own parents, children, or spouse; if necessary, He said, you should leave those family members behind to follow Him. On one occasion, He even forbade a man from attending his own father's funeral. See, for several examples, Luke 9:59-62, Luke 12:51-53, and Luke 14:25-26.

- He claimed to see and converse with angels. See Mark 1:12-13.

- He practiced civil disobedience by refusing to answer the authorities' questions after He was arrested. See Matthew 27:11-14.

- He called those who disagreed with Him liars and children of the devil. See John 8:42-45.

- He claimed to have known Abraham, who lived two thousand years before Jesus was born. See John 8:51-58.

- He willingly sacrificed His own life, believing that by His death He could save us all. See Luke 23:33-46.

THIS WEEK'S MEDITATION:

"Help me free Jesus particularly and other great spiritual leaders generally from their exile to the unread pages of dusty books, from the rote dogmas of superficial faith, and from the idolatry of political tracts. Let me understand these seers for what they truly were: radical, demanding, complex believers struggling against a world they considered nuts. Let me weigh their demands and teachings in all their stark zealotry, and know that I've been weighed, too, and found wanting."

JESUS SPOKE
FAITH-FILLED WORDS

Jesus pretty much invented the doctrine of faith. When you read the biblical biographies about Him, it's amazing how many times, and in how many contexts, Jesus talks about the importance of humans focusing their belief upon the proper object.

To understand how radical a notion that was, consider that in the Old Testament—the thirty-nine books that make up the Hebrew Scriptures, the only Bible with which most of Jesus' listeners would have been familiar—the word "faith" appears only twice.

Yet "faith" was perhaps the central term in Jesus' vocabulary. Later, His disciples referred to "faith" hundreds of times as they composed the theological biographies, letters, and other writings that became the New Testament. Faith, Jesus taught, gets God's attention and ignites His power. It enables the sick to recover and the dead to rise.

Matthew tells us about two blind men who followed Jesus into a house, hoping He would restore their sight.

"Do you believe I can do this?" Jesus asked.

"Yes," they said.

"Then it will be done according to your faith," He replied.

The men's sight returned.

Matthew also recounts how Jesus invited Peter to walk with Him across the surface of a windy sea. After a few steps, Peter lost his nerve and sank into the waves.

Jesus fished Peter out. "You have so little faith," Jesus said. "Why did you doubt?"

Jesus had trouble comprehending why everyone couldn't walk across the sea. To Him, it was simply a matter of knowing God's personality and trusting His power.

Jesus and the New Testament's authors understood faith to be a key attribute of God's own character. Because we humans are made in God's image, they said, we should imitate Him by learning to operate by faith, too.

For instance, Saint Paul, in his letter to the Christians at Rome, describes God as the one who "speaks into existence that which is not." Thus, God Himself acts by faith. God sees a negative as if it's a positive—and talks to it accordingly. Another New Testament writer says the cosmos was created from nothing when God spoke to the nothingness. God simply believed that what He said would come to pass, against all odds.

You might have noticed a second dynamic at work here. For God, and for Jesus, faith is connected to speaking. In the Bible, God formed the planets and stars from nothing by talking to the vacuum. Similarly, when Jesus wanted to calm a storm, He spoke to it in faith: "Peace! Be still!" The storm hushed. "Out of the heart's abundance, the mouth speaks," He explained.

In the gospels we find Jesus trying to teach His disciples how they can perform such feats. He says, "If you have faith the size of a tiny mustard seed, you can say to this mountain, 'Move from here to there,' and it will go. Nothing will be impossible to you."

Again, you see, for Jesus the principle involved combining a faith-filled heart with faith-filled words—to unleash supernatural, creative power.

Our first reaction might be, "Well, that was easy enough for Him. He was the Son of God!"

Notably, though, in his letter to Rome Saint Paul adds that every human inherently possesses a portion of faith. God doesn't send us into the world unequipped.

Indeed, common sense tells us that no human society could function without faith. I've managed to stay married in part because I believe that when I'm away from home on business, my wife isn't entertaining other men in our bed. She has faith that I'm not consorting with call girls in a distant city. You work long hours at your office because you believe that at the end of the week your boss will hand you a check to compensate you for your efforts; you haven't actually seen this week's check, but you know it will be there at the proper time. Sailors aboard an aircraft carrier calmly endure ocean storms because they trust the seaworthiness of their ship and the competence of their captain.

Generally speaking, all these things come to pass just as we've trusted they will. We've had dealings before with our wives, bosses, and ships. We know their characters and their histories. Occasionally we're fooled and disappointed, but not often.

So we do have faith, and it's based on our experiences.

But in the Bible Jesus seems to be upset frequently by the direction in which the people around Him have aimed their trust. Once, after He's rescued his disciples from a storm at sea, He asks them, "Where is your faith?"

The question implies that these men did possess faith, but that they'd misdirected it. The men believed only what they could see. They initially had faith in their boat, until the waves started battering it. Then they shifted their faith to the storm. The waves looked more powerful than the boat, so they believed they were doomed.

For Jesus, always, there existed One more powerful and more reliable than any ship or storm—and every bit as real.

But that One is invisible, a Spirit. We can't see Him with human eyes. We only can see Him by making a diligent, ongoing effort to get to know Him, by experiencing His very real power over and again.

I think that's what bothered Jesus. The men tossed at sea didn't trust God to rescue them because they hadn't bothered to develop a friendship with Him beforehand, a relationship of trust. Faith in God comes from knowing Him.

I'm not going to claim that you and I could literally walk across a lake or that we could stop a hurricane if we'd just talk with God more often and choose our words more carefully. But we might be amazed by what we could do, by the power we would release, by the wonders that would flow from us.

THIS WEEK'S MEDITATION:

"Lord, fill my heart with faith in You. Train my mouth to speak words of trust and deliverance wherever I find myself."

LIFE MULTIPLIES
FROM DEATH

Jesus was crucified at age thirty-three. How, we might ask, could one who died so young in so obscure a place have birthed a religion that's still around?

John's gospel includes a passage that I think helps unlock this mystery. Just before He is arrested and murdered, Jesus says to his followers: "Unless a grain of wheat falls into the ground and dies, it abides alone. But if it dies, it brings forth much fruit. He who loves his life shall lose it. He who hates his life in this world shall keep it to eternal life."

The message: God redeems life from various kinds of deaths. But if we humans selfishly cling to our own comfort and safety, or even if we harbor the past injustices done to us—if in any form we refuse to "die" to self—we block this divine process.

The Christian faith was born in tragedy: Jesus' unjust execution. God resurrected Him three days later, and through Him has been quickening new life in men and women since. First, though, Jesus had to fall. Every resurrection is preceded by a death.

That paradox remains at work all around us today, in a variety of ways.

I have a friend, Rex Martin, who was sentenced to three years in prison for his role in some burglaries. Rex had been a proud, stubborn guy. But jail broke him. Through desperate tears, he begged God to take control of his life and redeem good from it.

During his ordeal, Rex was held for months in our county's detention center. I often visited him there, trying to encourage his budding faith. Once I brought with me another minister, John Rohrer, who possesses an uncanny ability to discern God's plans. John talked with Rex over a phone in the narrow visiting room. Rex sat on the other side of a thick security glass. "God's going to free you from this place," John predicted. "When you come out, you'll bring with you a multitude of souls."

I didn't think much about it at the time. But I kept looking for ways to help Rex. I decided that the church where I'm a pastor could start a ministry to the jail's inmates, including Rex. The jailer agreed to allow a few of our members to come once a week and hold services. Ironically, as soon as our weekly ministry began, Rex was granted shock probation and released.

The worship services continued. Today, 25 percent of the county's inmates attend our church's crowded jail services. Many have been dramatically transformed. It's incredible to watch, and it all grew from that sorry episode in Rex's young life.

Rex surrendered his personal tragedy to God; he "died" to his ego and false sense of self-sufficiency. God then used his incarceration to deliver redemption to dozens of others.

Or consider this example. A few years ago, my dad bought several used bicycles at yard sales and fixed them good as new.

Before Christmas he anonymously phoned into a call-in show on our small town's radio station. He announced that he'd give nice secondhand bicycles to parents who wanted bikes for Christmas presents to their kids but couldn't afford to buy them.

The response was enormous. He'd tapped into a real need. So Dad kept doing this each Christmas. Each year he distributed more bikes than the year before.

Gradually Dad quit donating used bicycles and started giving brand-new ones.

Word leaked out. A local business group offered to match whatever money Dad raised for the project through private donations. The local newspaper wrote a front-page story. Last Christmas Dad was able to give away more than seventy new bikes.

But the source of Dad's generosity is wretched pain. He grew up destitute. Even in his sixties, Dad barely can talk about his childhood without crying, so he doesn't discuss it much. I know that Christmas wasn't much of an affair at his house. He and his siblings were lucky if they got an orange or some candy.

When he was ten, Dad started working. He bought himself a succession of old claptrap bicycles. The fender came off one as he sped down a hill, hit the front tire, and locked it up. He flipped over the handlebars, knocking out a tooth.

Poverty left both physical and emotional marks on Dad, but he turned his grief to positive ends. As an older man he decided he could prevent a few kids from having to ride junky bikes like the ones he'd had as a boy. He might save a couple of teeth.

155

So, because one child grew up during the Depression suffering the indignities wrought by poverty and decrepit bicycles, scores of children now are riding shiny new bikes. From Dad's pain, God bloomed scores of joyful deeds.

Jesus' own life was a lot like that. Who could have had a tougher time?

His mother was unmarried when she became pregnant with Him. He was born poor. A despot drove Him and His parents from their home country. Tradition says Jesus' stepfather died when He was a teenager, leaving Him to support His siblings. Jesus' relatives accused Him of being crazy. He grew up under the brutal rule of a foreign army. Religious zealots persecuted Him for His beliefs.

He might have become a sociopath, bent on avenging the wrongs done Him. He might have recruited an army of terrorists.

Instead He became the Prince of Peace. Clearly, Jesus had surrendered the vicissitudes of His life to God long before He surrendered Himself to a cross to save us.

To some extent, everyone similarly has been kicked around. We ourselves decide whether our misfortunes will make us generous or stingy, whether we'll trust God or rail against Him, whether we'll forgive or let bitterness fester in our hearts like an infection.

We choose the legacies we'll leave. If we stingily hoard either our measly comforts or our petty resentments, we'll die alone and forgotten. If we relinquish the good and bad to God, if we "die" to ourselves, abundant life can multiply from our tombs.

THIS WEEK'S MEDITATION:

"As I progress on this long journey of little deaths, help me surrender my fate to You. Plant me as a seed— and grow blessings from me."

FATHERHOOD IS EQUAL PARTS LOVE AND PAIN

The cold March evening in 1956 that my mother went into labor, my dad sat up all night in a small-town hospital, waiting for me.

He did, I suppose, what dads did in those days: He held my mother's hand; tried unsuccessfully to nap on uncomfortable couches; anxiously walked darkened hospital corridors to peer through windows into the black, cold night.

Anyway, the night passed as my dad waited helplessly. By ten o'clock the next morning, haggard, he had stepped across the street for coffee when I finally arrived.

My birth was a difficult one. In the process, my malleable skull was mashed badly out of shape and my skin was bruised.

When my father returned from his cup of coffee and was given a peek at me, he thought I was grotesquely and permanently deformed. Fear and fatigue overcame him. He wept at my ugliness.

Fortunately, the injury wasn't as bad as it first seemed. Like most babies, I was surprisingly resilient. Within a day or two my skull returned to a normal shape and the bruises faded.

My father's moment of anguish was transformed with my

skull. That awful moment when he first saw me became a family joke—a laughter born of relief, a story my father still tells more than forty years later.

"You talk about ugly babies," he'll say. "When Paul was born he was so ugly I cried." (Some wag invariably adds that I haven't changed much.)

I've long since become father to a son of my own. And in one of those paradoxes that happen among family generations, I had my own anguish. John's birth, like mine, was fraught with difficulty.

Medical technology had changed, of course, by 1983. I was watching the fetal monitor attached to our unborn child's skull when I saw his heartbeat plunge nearly to near zero. I rushed into the hall and called a nurse. She read the monitor, then dashed out for our doctor. Together they worked until they restored the baby's heartbeat. It was a long, long night.

Then, in the delivery room, in the last dark hours before sunup, the birth at last almost over, I saw the obstetrician suddenly blanch. He glanced at the nurse assisting him, and her eyes widened above her surgical mask.

Our baby, it turned out, was being born compound. His foot had lodged under his chin as he entered the birth canal, constricting his oxygen supply. That's what had caused his heart rate to dip.

For a long moment, the doctor simply sat there and stared, not knowing quite what to do. Finally, taking a chance, he grabbed the forceps and pulled, literally, for dear life.

159

The moment I saw our son, I knew he was hurt. He seemed to be breathing okay, but, because of the position he'd been in, pulling him through the birth canal had wrenched his legs horribly apart. His right leg flopped sickeningly outward, like a frog's leg. As the doctor worked over my wife, the nurse rushed our child to a crib on the other side of the room. The baby wailed as she worked his leg to see how bad the damage was.

Another doctor came into the room, also went pale, and said he thought our son's hip was broken.

I discovered how instantly black visions of the future can course through a parent's mind: I saw my boy's childhood filled with painful operations, leg braces, a debilitating limp. For the first time, I knew the consuming terror, the unspeakable pain in my father's first glimpse of me.

Fortunately, in another of those generational coincidences, it turned out the fear was unnecessary. As they worked over our child they soon discovered his hip was not broken. Within hours he looked as healthy as any baby, his tiny legs kicking strong and true.

Also, as in my birth, that moment of helpless agony became something of a joke. When he was younger I sometimes kidded John about his having been born with frogs' legs. He thought that was a funny thing. He'd cackle.

Today, he's momentarily too sophisticated—in his own estimation—to see the humor in such a childish joke. He's taller than I am. He expends most of his energy trying to figure out how he can impress teenage girls.

But often I watch him as he's loping across the backyard on

solid legs, or tossing a football with his cousins, or flirting with a neighborhood girl, and I think back to the truth of that first night we passed together.

I think about the love that carried me through hours of ordeal in a labor room and a delivery room with my wife. It's the same love that made my father last through an equally long night and that brought him to tears the next morning.

I think about the agony that is blended with love, that is part of love. And rarely do I watch my son without also breathing a silent word of thanksgiving—for him.

For two strong legs.

And for my dad, who was with me from the first moments of my life, and who is with me yet—who has taught me that no child can be blessed with a greater inheritance than to have a father who stays through the worst and hopes for the best.

THIS WEEK'S MEDITATION:

"Lord, You have made this promise to us: 'I will never desert you, nor will I ever forsake you.' Strengthen me that I would never desert nor forsake my child, regardless of how painful love might sometimes be."

MY SON TAKES
HIS TURN AT BAT

In preparing this book, I spent much time sorting through my past: old newspaper columns I'd written, sermon notes and journals. Some of what I found embarrassed me. It was too personal or inept or vain, and I was glad to forget those words. I found other pieces that still moved me, that evoked special periods I wish I could revisit.

What follows is one of the latter, a column I wrote for the *Lexington Herald-Leader* in 1994. I decided not to tamper with it. But I have added a postscript of sorts and, as always, a meditation.

My son, eleven, is walking up the stairs at home. He stops and looks down at me.

"You know what?" he says.

"What?"

"Sometimes at night when I'm in bed? I start thinking about you. And then I start crying."

"Oh?" I don't recall our having had a fuss recently. "You're crying because you're mad?"

"No. Because I love you so much."

"Well, that's odd," I say. "Sometimes I do the very same thing, thinking about you."

My son is virtually a straight-A student. But halfway through his fifth-grade year, he brings home a report card bearing a B in, of all things, reading.

I have two college degrees in English. Books are vital to me.

I don't expect him always to make A's, I say. But reading is the most important subject because you have to read well to study anything else. He says he understands.

The next grading period, unfazed, he walks in with a C in reading. We have another talk, more pointed. We spend hours reading aloud.

The final grading period of the year arrives. Another C.

My wife and I help chaperon his class's year-end trip to Pigeon Forge, Tennessee, and to Dollywood amusement park. He's popular, I discover. Boys playfully jostle him. Girls hover over him like hummingbirds.

There's another child, though, who seems to be left alone every time the kids choose up partners for roller-coaster rides.

My son notices this, too. As we stand in line for yet another ride, he leaves the pack and walks up to this boy, drapes an arm over his shoulder.

"Hey, can I ride with you?" my son says.

When we return from the trip, I ask: "In your class, who's your best friend? Kyle? Alan?"

"Wendi," he says.

We're watching TV. It's his bedtime. He tells me good night. I think of how fast our lives are changing.

"I'm so proud of you," I say.

Silence.

"I'm proud of you," I repeat, thinking he didn't hear me.

He says, "Uh . . . I love you."

Obviously, he assumes that I expect him to say he's proud of me as well. And he isn't.

"Why aren't you proud of me?" I ask.

"I guess because you're not rich or famous or anything."

"I see. Could it be that your priorities are off a bit?"

He shrugs.

As calmly as I can, I explain the things that I believe really matter: that I spend time with him, that I respect his mom.

"Someday," I say, "you may decide that I'm a better dad than you think I am now."

Or maybe he won't.

The next morning as I arrive at work, the phone is ringing.

"Dad?"

He's never called me at the office before. Ever.

"Dad?" His voice is tiny. "I'm sorry if I hurt your feelings."

"Well, I'm a big guy."

He sobs into the phone.

"Daddy, I am proud of you."

When I was his age, I rode my pony at a dead gallop. On a football field, I'd knock you out of your shoes. But I loathed playing baseball. Too boring.

My son adores baseball.

Still, he's so lackadaisical—or worse, perhaps, timid. When he faces a pitcher, he rarely swings at the ball. He watches it whip through the strike zone as if he's a curious spectator.

So I'm attending my umpteenth hot, dusty game. My son's at bat. He has two strikes. "You can't hit the ball if you won't swing the bat!" I yell.

The pitcher winds up. The throw is wild. My son swings and strikes out. I realize I've become one of those crazed dads coaching from the stands. The kind I hate.

We also have a new phenomenon at these games. Wendi.

She rides to the ballpark with us. She's smart. She's sweet.

But I'm not ready for this.

At the games, Wendi mostly sits with her chin on her palms. She sighs glumly.

"You like baseball?" I ask finally.

She looks at me as if I just asked whether she likes hip-replacement surgery.

"Me neither," I say. Then I add, "I guess we're both here for the same reason."

At that moment, my son trots from the far side of his team's dugout, whirring a baseball bat at the motionless air. Our conversation halts. Our chins rise.

My fingers crossed in hope, I watch him step to the plate.

Much has changed since the *Herald-Leader* published that column. John is now fifteen. By the time you read this he'll be sixteen and driving a car, a thought that strikes terror in my heart.

He stands more than six feet tall. He quit playing baseball a couple of years ago and devotes most of his time to other pursuits in which I had no interest as a teenager: speech tournaments and school plays. I try to work up an interest.

He's generally a well-adjusted kid, I think, and quite well behaved, but he no longer talks with me as openly as he did a few years ago; he communicates mainly through grunts. His grades remain A's and B's, but he's as indifferent a student as you'll ever find.

Some things, though, never change. I still get teary as I lie in my bed staring at a dark ceiling, thinking of how much he means to me. I'm still proud of him.

I've still got my fingers crossed.

"Lord, children are the most valuable gift You ever give us. Nothing I can do in life is as important as teaching my son well— for in doing that I will affect generations to come. Help me, God, to raise him right. I'm so flawed, and the job is so complicated."

Week

THE HIGH COST OF TRUTH

Linda Emery was a good nurse. But that year had been a terrible one. In May, her grandmother had died. In June, Linda's mother, who lived in Florida, had suffered a heart attack. She was lingering near death.

Though Linda didn't know it, she was herself seriously anemic due to complications from surgery she'd undergone a few years before. A divorced mother, she also was struggling to pay medical bills from her operation and its related illnesses, as well as debts from her education.

So, that summer of 1985, to earn extra money, Linda had begun pulling overtime at the large Catholic hospital where she already worked the night shift on the cancer ward. She hired out as a private duty nurse, too.

Her two children, then fourteen and ten, resented her being gone so much. They started acting up, intentionally keeping her awake during the day when she usually slept.

Linda discovered she wasn't invincible. She lost her concentration at work.

About 6:00 A.M. on an August Saturday, Linda was told that a leukemia patient on her floor had pulled loose the I.V. tube in his heart catheter. She left another patient, who was vomiting blood, and rushed to the man's room to replace the I.V.

The procedure required her to flush the man's catheter with sodium chloride. Because several of his family members were trying to sleep in the room, Linda didn't turn on the light. Exhausted and harried, she pulled a bottle of medicine from the patient's box of catheter supplies, which normally contained sodium chloride. She looked at the label in the room's half-light, saw "chloride."

She double-checked. Saw "chloride" again.

She injected him.

The man grabbed his chest, pain bulging his eyes. He quit breathing. Linda jerked back on the syringe, dropped the bottle, and started CPR.

She yelled for a nurse's aide to call a "code." Other hospital workers raced to help her. Together, they managed to bring the patient back—but he was left comatose.

A doctor said a blood clot probably had lodged in the fellow's heart.

"I feel like I did something" to him, Linda said.

An hour later, she returned to the patient's room. The debris scattered during the frantic minutes of the "code"—needles, tubes, medicine packages—already had been swept up. But, on instinct, Linda knelt to feel around the floor.

She found a bottle that had rolled under the bed. She picked it up. Flinched.

Linda couldn't believe what its label said. Potassium chloride, not sodium chloride. Squirting that full strength into some-body was like shooting liquid fire into him. Undiluted potassium chloride normally wasn't kept on the cancer ward. How it had wound up in her patient's catheter kit never became clear.

But no one had caught her accident.

When her shift ended, Linda kept silent and went home. "I didn't want to believe I had done that," she said later. "I didn't want to think about that."

She had children to feed. If she confessed she would lose her job. She might lose her nurse's license.

For several days, Linda tried to rationalize the accident. The patient was elderly. He'd been terminally ill before the accident. Nothing would be gained by her telling what she'd done. But she was so miserable she couldn't even pray—and as a devout Presbyterian her relationship with God was the most important thing in her life.

Every day when she came to work, she saw the comatose man's family keeping watch over him. Before the accident, they'd been scheduled to take him home so he could die in peace with-out running up more medical bills. Now he lay unconscious, kept alive by tubes, the bills mounting.

Linda went to see her pastor and confessed. The pastor said, "Truth must prevail. Because having a clear conscience in the sight of God is of the utmost."

She began thinking of ways out. Her vacation was scheduled to start in a few days. If she could hold out until then, she would go to Florida, find another job, tend her mother, and just never come back to Kentucky. "I was falling apart," she said.

Finally she told her secret to a couple who were friends from her church. The husband volunteered to go with her to her hospital superiors. That was the final nudge she needed. "I can't live in a spiritual wasteland," she said.

She was trembling and chalk white as they rode the elevator up to see Linda's bosses. Her friend insisted God would deliver Linda for her honesty.

Linda knew better. When she confessed she was suspended on the spot.

The other nurses on her shift that night had baked a birthday cake to give her. She never got it. The patient she'd injected died the next day—as if God had released him.

A few days after that Linda officially was fired.

She took work as an office temporary, as a grocery store clerk. Her income dropped from $25,000 a year to $7,000. Her children went from eating name-brand cereals to eating oatmeal. Linda sought counseling. She managed—"with a lot of prayer"—to cope. In February 1986, the state nursing board placed Linda on two years' probation and fined her $250.

Eventually, after months of living in a probationary limbo, she was hired by a mental hospital as a psychiatric nurse, a less stressful job than a cancer ward. She was assigned to the day shift, which allowed her to rest at night and to spend time with her children. She quit working overtime.

Her probation expired. Slowly she put herself and her career back together. She'd trudged through the fiery furnace and finally had walked out—singed, but alive.

Linda also became active in Nurses Assisting Nurses, an organization in which nurses counsel and support one another. She found to her surprise that people there looked up to her for her honesty. Other medical workers told her they'd made mistakes similar to hers, but hadn't confessed. Because their consciences haunted them, some drank too much. Several had developed marital difficulties.

Linda realized her new friends were paying higher prices for their errors than she'd paid. The wrongs they'd kept hidden chronically gnawed at their guts.

"The damage I think it does to the soul is incalculable," she said of these secret sins. "People can't resolve the guilt they feel."

She understood her friends' dilemma. She knew their fear of telling the truth about their errors.

"There's something to be said about doing right," Linda admitted. "It's sometimes real tough."

But not as tough as trying to hide your guilt forever, she decided. For Linda, retaining a clear conscience had turned out to be worth more than all she'd lost. It had broken her pride and emptied her pocketbook—but it had freed her soul.

"I'm not scared anymore," she said.

*"Give me the courage to tell the truth, no matter the cost.
Lying is, in the long run, far more expensive."*

MINISTERS ARE
ONLY HUMAN

A Southern Baptist preacher visited me. He'd been in the ministry four decades and was near retirement. But when he arrived at my office he was wounded emotionally, financially, and spiritually. His congregation had turned him out.

Apparently, some parishioners didn't think the church's membership or revenues were growing sufficiently. I guess the preacher couldn't find the right marketing strategy.

So the congregation just got rid of him. At his age, he was finding it difficult to get a new pastorate. He and his wife had been forced by need to sell their house.

Churches have changed, he told me. When he was a young pastor, congregations were more interested in spiritual matters. Back then, a minister's job was to minister: preach the good news, counsel the distressed, hold the hands of the dying.

Now, he said, churches are being run like secular businesses.

His first inkling of a shift in members' expectations had come years earlier. A lay leader of his church, a corporate manager by trade, had arrived at his office and demanded to see the productivity reports. The preacher didn't know what the guy was talking about.

Soon another lay leader asked him, "Preacher, how many people do you preach to on Sunday morning?"

"About seven hundred," the pastor replied.

"That's seven hundred man-hours," the guy said. "Don't waste one of them."

It's possible that this minister was just lousy at his job.

But one survey of 3,200 Baptists by seminary researchers seems to confirm what he said. It found that Baptists now "hold high expectations of their pastors and want them to be proficient in every area of pastoral ministry," a Baptist Press article reported.

The pollsters asked 108 questions about what qualities were important in a minister. Church members wanted all 108. They expected their pastors to act like corporate chief executive officers. They also wanted ministers to have flawless personal characters, to be personally pious, and to get along well with people. They expected the preachers to be "program-oriented" and committed to conservative causes.

Used to be, a Christian preacher's main job was to point people to Jesus Christ. Evidently, congregations now want the preacher to be Jesus Christ.

This shift cuts across denominations. It's apparent in other faiths, too.

Maybe it has something to do with the increased affluence of U.S. churchgoers. A half century ago, the vast majority of

Americans weren't college-educated. They worked at manual labor. They were trying to escape the successive blights of a Depression, a World War, and a worsening Cold War.

Perhaps lay folks then were more grateful for the heartening presence of an honest, conscientious minister. Perhaps they were more tolerant of a preacher's shortcomings, because they were more aware of their own and the world's.

Today, more lay members are educated, success-oriented, and spoiled. They want the church to be run like any profitable company.

But a church isn't primarily a business, even if it does collect money and construct buildings. Supposedly a Christian congregation, to cite my own faith, is an arm of the body of Christ. If so, it should be merciful. It should extend that mercy to its own pastor.

Another time a businesswoman, an active layperson in her Lutheran church, came to see me. Tears welled in her eyes. Her pastor had gotten into a tiff with a subordinate on the church's staff, who then resigned. The dispute basically amounted to a personality conflict, but the pastor had acted arbitrarily and with an ill temper, my friend thought.

"What do I do now?" she asked. "I don't want to go to Sunday services anymore. All anybody can talk about is what a jerk the minister is. And I agree."

I advised her to forgive her pastor, return to church, and keep her mouth shut.

I'm not sure she liked my advice. But having observed countless congregational squabbles from multiple perspectives—as the son of a pastor, as a young layman, as a religion journalist, and as a pastor myself—I find my sympathies almost always lie with the ministers. They're not always right, but they labor under nearly impossible expectations.

So allow me to offer these reminders:

First, ministers are human. That should be obvious, but it's shocking how many people forget it. To some parishioners the pastor or rabbi is very nearly God incarnate. They think ministers live on some special spiritual plane where they hold face-to-face conferences with the Almighty. When the minister screws up, these folks are shattered. Often they turn on him and devour him in their anguish.

Then there's another variety of congregational members, the self-righteous lot, who assume that all preachers are expendable dunderheads. This group turns minor idiosyncrasies—the pastor shows up for choir practice in a polo shirt instead of a clerical collar, say—into major moral brouhahas.

Both groups place unbearable burdens on clergy. Frequently the clergy overreact by trying to behave perfectly, by trying to hide their faults even from themselves.

Inevitably they fail, because ministers, like everyone else, are imperfect. They might be marvelous speakers but lousy administrators. They might abstain from bourbon but have an uncontrollable passion for hot fudge sundaes or disco music.

Everyone would do well to recognize that ahead of time and be prepared for it.

Second, ministers need emotional support. Unhappy with the rabbi? Invite her out to lunch—and pay the tab. Tell her how much you appreciate her. You might be surprised at how much a little encouragement will accomplish.

Third, ministers occasionally need loving correction. The emphasis here is on "loving," not on "correction." Most clergy really want to keep as many parishioners happy as possible. So if the priest has hurt you, tell him. But do it kindly, in the spirit of: "I care about you, but I'm disappointed. I may be at fault myself. How can we can constructively work through this together?"

Fourth, conflicts are opportunities for spiritual growth. Too often, laypeople caught in a congregational dispute simply flee to another church—or fire their pastor. Rarely is anyone served by either action. When trouble arises, stick it out. One sign of maturity is the ability to stand fast during hard times. Besides, if you go to another church, you'll soon discover it has as many problems as the church you left. I promise.

And don't dump the minister unless he's an utter lunatic or a degenerate. You don't need a perfect pastor. You're not there to worship him. You're there to worship God.

THIS WEEK'S MEDITATION:

"Let me show members of the clergy the same amounts of mercy, patience, and understanding that I expect to receive from them. Let me remember to worship You, not other humans."

CHAIN OF COMMAND

I don't like being told what to do.

For instance, I've always loved to read. Even as a boy I'd read anything for pleasure: cereal boxes, newspapers, novels, biographies, psychology textbooks, even poetry. I can hardly remember a moment when I didn't have a paper, magazine, or book in my hands.

So in college I decided to major in English literature. People who major in English, I knew, get to read books almost nonstop, and receive college credit for it.

But once I'd embarked on my course of study, I discovered an uncomfortable glitch in my own personality. The moment a professor assigned a book and told our class to finish it by, say, next Thursday—I instantly lost all interest in reading it.

Knowing that I had to read it made me not want to. Some part of me just didn't want to be told what to do, even if the request was perfectly reasonable.

There is within the heart of most humans, I imagine, a similar germ of rebellion. Each of us has a bit of the devil in his soul, and the devil is, more than anything, a rebel.

We don't like to be ordered around by our parents when we're young or by cops when we're grown.

How many people have you heard shout in anger, "Ain't nobody gonna tell me what to do!" Graveyards and prisons are full of such fools.

The Scriptures tell us that to attain lengthy, happy, and prosperous lives, we must humble ourselves before the proper authorities, whether they're heavenly or earthly.

That's how we maintain order in society and in our souls. Rebels make life miserable for everyone else. They disrupt traffic and sow public distrust. They also ruin themselves. Often they want to be exalted as role models, or hope to be perceived as hip, but mostly they lead pretty awful lives. Typically they become paranoid, always looking over their shoulders for the authorities, even when the authorities aren't after them. Sometimes they're drug addicts. Many are nihilists; they rebel because they don't believe in anything and their lives have no meaning to them. They're mad at the world and assume the world's mad at them.

There's yet another reason why we're to respect authority. Until we learn to act properly while under the authority of others, we can't perform properly when we're placed in authority ourselves, as most of us will be from time to time, whether as parents at home or teachers at school.

The Bible points out several kinds of leaders to whom each of us is expected to submit:

God. He's the ultimate authority, of course. If you can't submit to Him, you rarely will submit to anyone else, either, except by force.

Family members. We're to obey our parents when we're young and honor our spouses after we marry. Whether you're a man, a woman, or a child, you're to become a selfless servant to those in your own household.

Church leaders. Pastors, music leaders, teachers, and others in key roles are to be treated with the utmost respect. To dishonor or criticize them is to dishonor and criticize God, who called them despite their human frailties.

Our bosses at work. Saint Paul warns that when we're on the job, we're not really working for the man or woman who ranks above us—we're working for the Lord. We're to treat our managers with the same respect we would give God.

Civil authorities. Saints Paul and Peter both caution us that God has placed the rulers of the state in their positions. Thus we should obey them, except when following them would mean directly disobeying God's laws. Paul and Peter wrote this while living under the dominion of evil, pagan Roman despots who frequently persecuted the church.

Which leads to my final point. Our duty to honor those in authority has virtually nothing to do with whether we happen to like or agree with them.

Of course there are limits to every rule. There are severe situations when rebellion is justified. If your parents sexually abuse you, you certainly have a right to resist and to report them to the police. If your employer demands that you bribe a foreign official, you should resign; bribery not only is immoral, it's a felony. If your husband tries to hit you in the head with a hammer, feel free to run for your life. If your government starts gassing Jews or disabled people or labor unionists, you're duty bound to protest loudly.

Most problems, though, aren't nearly that severe. Mainly, we're to submit to the powers above us, the idea being that perhaps God has placed all of us where we are. The boss may be a jerk, but she's still the boss—and maybe God has set her in the office she holds, perhaps to sand off some of our own rough edges.

In bowing to the proper authorities, we accomplish three things. We help keep society in order, we sow peace in our own lives, and we prepare ourselves to lead.

THIS WEEK'S MEDITATION:

"I will practice looking at those in positions of authority over me as if they might be instruments of God. I'll ask myself this: 'What's God trying to tell me through this mayor? My boss? My spouse? My parents?' I'll look within myself to see if I can root out the seeds of ungodly rebellion."

WE REDISCOVER PRAYER DURING TROUBLED TIMES

I once saw a T-shirt that said, "In case of nuclear war, the Supreme Court ban on prayer in schools will be lifted." That's trite, but it contains a nugget of truth.

When life is easy, we humans tend to ignore religion. But let bullets zing by and even the least spiritual of us suddenly turns pious. It's the phenomenon called "foxhole religion."

As the world geared up for the Gulf War in 1991, when the war's outcome lay in the future and remained anyone's guess, both houses of the Kentucky legislature hurriedly passed a resolution recognizing "the supreme authority and just government of Almighty God in all the affairs of men and nations."

The resolution, introduced by two state lawmakers who also happened to be ordained ministers, called "the citizens of the commonwealth to prayer, fasting, confession of national transgressions." It was modeled after an 1863 proclamation by Abraham Lincoln.

At the national level during the Gulf crisis, President Bush met with the Reverend Billy Graham and with his own Episcopal bishop. Bush publicly asked for Americans to pray hard.

Politicians' motives are always suspect, of course. Bush may be deeply religious. Or he may have been appealing to religion because, well, if you're going to send people's sons and daughters off to war, it helps if everyone knows God is on your side. Even Saddam Hussein started quoting the Koran during those nerve-jangling weeks.

However, this prayer instinct isn't confined to politicians or preachers. Rank-and-file Americans also found new fervor as the crisis in the Middle East escalated. Across the country church attendance jumped dramatically.

I've asked several people why this always happens during wars and natural disasters. Psychologically speaking, one theory goes, humans need to create moral structures for troublesome events. It helps us ward off our terror. Fear breeds on uncertainty, and religion helps provide certain answers.

Sounds impressive, but it's not totally satisfying.

Other people have told me they see a recurring move of the Almighty.

"Historically," said one of the Kentucky legislators who helped draft the state's Gulf War prayer resolution, "we have been reminded by famine, pestilence, and war . . . of our great need for God."

The Bible itself agrees that God ordains the rise and fall of nations, from which people learn "that they should seek God, in the hope that they might feel after Him and find Him." When we do seek God, we discover that "He is not far from any of us. For in Him we live and move and have our being."

Yet that's troublesome, too. If you follow the idea to its logical end, it sounds as if God manipulates—or even creates—the napalming of little children in war zones just to advance His own cause, that God prepares us to be cradled by His loving Spirit by first tossing us into an inferno. A tough notion with which to deal.

I don't pretend to know all the answers to these theological dilemmas, but personally I think our wartime cries for God's help probably reflect a mixture of both human and divine impulses.

Most of us carry within us a nagging feeling that we're not complete, not whole, a seminary psychology professor once told me. I agree with him.

When things are going well, I suspect it's easy to suppress those nagging, universal insecurities. We busy ourselves with the temporal, with work and politics and family. We lie to ourselves. We say that we're masters of our own fates. Or we simply say nothing.

We ignore weighty and difficult issues such as eternity, goodness, peace, and justice—not out of malice, but out of preoccupation. In avoiding those subjects, we dig ourselves deeper into a "miry clay," as the old hymn says. It's a clay of uncharitable policies, self-absorption, and greed.

We hollow out mass graves one dollar, one workday, one election, one preoccupation at a time, all the while forgetting we're going to die.

That's mostly human nature, or psychology, if you prefer. We tend not to think about issues that make us nervous.

Finally, through our ignorance and neglect, our world breaks loose; we come face to face with the messes we've created and with how powerless we are to solve them. We realize we're not masters but ciphers. We reach for the infinite.

That's where I suspect we enter a largely spiritual realm. Ecclesiastes observes that God himself has put eternity into all human minds. Cover it, tarnish it, but it will still emerge. That seems to be so.

The urge to call on God is not limited to Americans or to the Judeo-Christian consciousness. In every nation, among every faith and people of no faith at all, humans cry out for divine aid in crises. The instinct transcends psychology or anthropology.

And in various ways, God answers when we call.

Yes, then, God is present in devastation. But it's hard to believe that God does those awful things to us to get our attention. No. We do them to ourselves. That's what we need to face.

Instead, we pray fervently during troubled times. Then, as soon as our difficulties pass, we forget the lesson we've learned.

Flannery O'Connor wrote a fictional story in which an old woman cries out to the Lord just as she is murdered by a sociopath, called The Misfit. After blasting her, the killer pontificates.

"She would of been a good woman," The Misfit says, "if it had been somebody there to shoot her every minute of her life."

Sadly, that describes most of us. If we spent as much time in prayer during peacetime as we do during war, we wouldn't have wars.

THIS WEEK'S MEDITATION:

"With all my heart, O God, I vow to call upon You as eagerly and sincerely during the good times as I do automatically during the bad."

PEOPLE NEED A
LITTLE PRAISE

Sometimes it's important to tell people how much they mean to us. We're quick to spout off when we're unhappy. It's praise we're stingy with. Maybe it's because we're scared. Hug a favorite coworker and you might be accused of sexual harassment. Call an old teacher and you might discover he doesn't even recall your name.

I'm glad for people who've made a leap of faith toward me, who risked looking stupid.

I remember attending my high school class's ten-year reunion. At twenty-eight, I was poor and working two, sometimes three, part-time jobs to make ends meet. My ego was lower than a snake's belly in a wagon rut. I kept all this to myself at the reunion. But all evening I was uncomfortable, wondering whether all my old pals could tell what a failure I'd been.

A few weeks later, I received a letter from one of the men I'd seen there, who'd been my best friend from the fifth grade through high school. He said how good it had been to talk with me, how much our years together as kids had meant. He was sorry, he wrote, that we had lost touch, and he just wanted me to know he was proud that he could say I was still his friend.

Men don't normally tell each other those kinds of things, even if we feel them in our hearts—at least small-town ex-jocks like us don't. But if my buddy Boyd had mailed me a thousand dollars, he couldn't have made me any happier. And I needed a thousand dollars.

Today, I'm sometimes asked to make speeches at churches, colleges, and civic clubs. I usually walk away feeling like I just laid a dozen pounds of bird droppings.

But because of another pal, Kenny, I feel at ease when I speak at my own church. He's a building contractor, a tanned, hard-muscled man you wouldn't expect to be free with compliments. Yet even if I bray like a jackass from the pulpit, Kenny will be the first person into the aisle afterward. He'll engulf my hand with his callused paw and pump it as if I were Billy Graham and the pope rolled into one.

"Paul, that was good," he'll say. "That helped me. Thanks, brother."

Next thing you know I'm strutting around like some silver-tongued orator. I'm smart enough to understand that Kenny probably has overstated my performance. Still the gift of those kind words does me good.

I've experimented myself with complimenting others. Compliments don't cost anything to give, but they can be like platinum to the person who receives them.

Once Sheila, one of my sisters-in-law, gave my son and me a ride home from a karate lesson. In several ways she's led a tough life. She grew up in a family frequently racked by tension. She's endured divorce and poverty. Worst, she lost her older son, Jason. He was severely brain damaged at birth, the result of a hospital accident during his delivery. He died at age nine.

As we rode along that day, for some reason she and I began talking about Jason. He'd been dead several years. To my surprise, Sheila emptied her heart to me. After Jason's death she'd nearly given up on herself and on the world, she said. For a long time she'd been furious with God. She'd also struggled with guilt; one relative had told her she was to blame for Jason's condition, that if she'd been closer to the Almighty her son wouldn't have been sick to begin with.

Mostly it was a one-sided conversation. I nodded a lot.

What can you say in the face of such loss? I understood why she'd found herself angry with God—but I also thought her fury might have destroyed her if she'd allowed it to continue unchecked. She hadn't done that, though; she'd pretty much worked through that part of her grief and was in church again. The relative who'd told her she was responsible for her son's illness had displayed an astounding insensitivity—but there was little I could do to erase the accusation or soothe the deep, automatic guilt any parent might feel after her child dies.

I did tell her what I could, the usual niceties and reassurances, but really I didn't feel qualified to counsel her, to offer my opinions, or even to have any opinions. Thank God, I haven't lost a child. I figured anything I could say about that experience would be self-evident or inadequate.

We pulled into my driveway. She shifted her van into park. We sat there in silence for a few moments.

I truly wanted to help. I felt she wanted me to help.

"Sheila," I blurted out finally, "you're one of the people I admire most in the world."

She stared at me. "What?"

I don't think that's what she was expecting.

"Yeah," I said. "You've been through more than almost anyone I know. If I were you I'd be locked in a padded cell. But you've never lost your mind. Instead, you've educated yourself and you're smart as a whip. You've held on to your faith, and you've even kept your sense of humor. You're so strong it's hard for me to comprehend."

Through her sunglasses, I saw tears brimming in her eyes.

I decided to quit while I was ahead. So I shut up.

"Thank you," she said. "Thank you."

That fast, she looked better. I could almost see the worry lines on her forehead relaxing.

As I stepped out of her van, I knew I'd witnessed, once again, the incredible power borne by a few simple words of praise.

THIS WEEK'S MEDITATION:

"Every day this week I will find at least one person to whom I can offer the treasure of lavish, heartfelt, and unexpected praise."

PROPHETS WITHOUT HONOR

Christian Rollin Emmitt was, he said, a prophet without honor in his own home. When he'd started out that week for Lexington, his wife had stayed behind at their home in Savannah. As Emmitt told it, she didn't possess a great deal of faith in the message he was proclaiming.

Fortunately, naysayers didn't bother him much. "I'm considered a heretic," he said. "I'm considered a Jesus freak by some. A fanatic. But I know that my redeemer liveth."

He'd been driving the countryside a quarter century, off and on, first in a converted school bus and, by the time I met him, in his "Roll-in Bible Chautauqua," a recreational vehicle covered by dozens of hand-painted signboards that proclaimed: "The study of magnetism" and "John 4:24: God is a Spirit: and they that worship Him must worship Him in spirit and in truth" and many other things as well.

Emmitt stood six foot three on legs thin as slats from a Venetian blind. He was seventy-five years old. His white mane and beard lifted gently on the afternoon breeze.

He was something of a signboard himself. His inexpensive shoes were black. When the sun hit his socks just right, the red

193

could momentarily blind you. His tattered pants and shirts were white. The shirts—he owned nearly twenty, he said—bore messages monogrammed on the backs, such as "I am a Christian. A soldier of Jesus Christ. II Timothy 2:1-6."

The black shoes represented his former sin, Emmitt said. Before he got saved in 1954, he'd been an alcoholic contemplating suicide. The socks were the color of Jesus' blood. The shirts and pants testified to the purity of his redeemed soul. Taken together, the clothes stood for his new life: "From darkness to light through the blood of Christ," Emmitt said.

He had gone on a fast earlier that year in Georgia, as a testimony. It had lasted thirty-five days, but ended when he came down with a cold. He was thinking of starting a new fast in Lexington—forty days seemed about right—if he could find a spot to park his RV that long.

His theology was a tad complex. I asked for specifics and got an answer that started with the symbolism he said was inherent in the design of corn, meandered through the similarity of the words "Adam" in Genesis and "atom" in physics, stopped off to visit the astronomer Ptolemy in A.D. 150, and ended with a lecture about the earth's tectonic plates. The logic appeared perfectly obvious to Emmitt, but I confess it eluded me.

This much I can say: I've never met a kinder host.

He spoke so softly it was difficult to hear him above the traffic whirring along the avenue near us. Emmitt had parked in an empty lot in a busy working-class neighborhood. I'd stopped to introduce myself.

In past years, Emmitt had broken both hips. He hobbled along with a crutch. Yet he repeatedly offered me the battered chair he'd lugged beneath a shade tree.

A police officer pulled up to check him out. Emmitt appeared glad to see him.

Emmitt used to be a Methodist who operated a dry-cleaning business in Savannah, he said after the officer left. In 1965, an audible voice told him to read the book of Genesis. Somehow—again, the connection wasn't clear—this voice had led to his split with Methodism and dry-cleaning.

Emmitt assured me that in the Bible, every catastrophe coincided with an alignment of our solar system's planets: "I've never had anyone challenge me with the Word about this."

He'd been to Chile fourteen times on mission trips. He was there in 1982, the last time the planets aligned. He camped in a pup tent on a mountain 12,500 feet above sea level and waited for the massive earthquake he expected to herald the beginning of the end for this world. But nothing happened.

"Stupid old Emmitt," he said.

After the disappointment in Chile, Emmitt had decided his calculations were off by eighteen years. Now he was sure the big quake would strike in the year 2000.

"I'm trying to warn the world—in a peaceful way," he said. That's why he was in Lexington. God had sent him to prepare us.

As we talked, a nicely dressed businessman drove up in a pickup. Evidently, he was the man who had granted Emmitt permission to park on the empty lot. He couldn't refuse, he explained sheepishly after noticing me standing off to one side. Emmitt looked a bit strange, but then people mocked Jesus, too.

"You never know," the guy said as he drove away.

Which expressed my sentiments precisely. The world always has been full of crackpots making apocalyptic predictions. As the millennium changes, and for a few years afterward, we'll likely hear from more and more of them.

The problem is that occasionally—usually in the least expected places—true prophets do happen along, too, sent by the Almighty. If we're not careful, we might classify them among the loonies.

The seer Isaiah walked around in public naked and barefoot for three years as a testimony against the spiritual nakedness of Egypt and Cush. John the Baptist lived in a desert, wore animal skins, and ate a diet of grasshoppers and honey. He was so weird that many of his contemporaries assumed him to be demon-possessed. But Jesus considered John the greatest prophet of them all.

I don't know whatever happened to Christian Rollin Emmitt. He and his RV disappeared from his lot shortly after I spent that instructive afternoon with him. I'd given him a business card, and he called once to say he'd moved to a new spot in the city. He wasn't sure exactly where he was. I never saw him again.

Maybe he was a nut. But then, maybe he wasn't. We'd be wise not to dismiss the Emmitts of our age too easily. One of them might turn out to be the real thing.

THIS WEEK'S MEDITATION:

"God, don't allow me to be misled by false prophets or fools. But give me the grace to know a real messenger when I see him."

HALLOWEENS VERSUS HALLELUJAHS

Halloween is near. Your jack-o'-lanterns are carved. Your children are assembling costumes for a night of trick-or-treating.

So, does this mean that you and your family are devil worshipers?

For some folks, it does. Increasingly, Halloween provokes more uneasiness than glee for many religious leaders—liberals and conservatives alike.

Some clergy claim the celebration's roots lie in the occult. They're correct. *The Encyclopaedia Britannica* says the holiday originated with the pagan Celtic festival Samhain, on which the devil was invoked for various divinations. "The souls of the dead were supposed to revisit their homes on this day," the *Britannica* says, "and the autumnal festival acquired sinister significance, with ghosts, witches, hobgoblins . . . and demons of all kinds said to be roaming about." Even today Halloween is the most important day of the year for contemporary witches, the *San Jose Mercury News* has reported.

Where I live, anything that even hints of the occult—particularly when it's practiced by young people—is suspect. There are reasons for this.

Not long ago, six young eastern Kentuckians who allegedly practiced Satanism slipped into Tennessee, where they abducted and shot four members of a family of Jehovah's Witnesses as they returned from a religious conference. Three of the victims died. The teenagers and young adults received life in prison without parole.

In western Kentucky, another group of teens who called themselves the Victorian Age Masquerade Society allegedly started out drinking blood, trying to become vampires. Several ended up charged in the double slaying of one member's parents. One boy in the group was linked to the theft and mutilation of puppies from an animal shelter.

As far as I know, Halloween wasn't a direct factor in these crimes. Still, you can understand why the occult makes a lot of folks around here squirm.

Besides, occult or not, the holiday is associated with all kinds of lesser mayhems, from throwing eggs at police cars to macabre public displays.

When I was a newspaper reporter, the executive director of the Kentucky Council of Churches—an interfaith, largely liberal alliance—went ballistic over a Halloween display at a store in a Lexington mall.

It consisted of a mock electric chair at the store's entrance, a life-size replica of the real thing with a dummy strapped into the hot seat. At posted times throughout each day the chair was activated. Fog rolled out. The ghoul in the chair writhed and moaned. A sign hung on yellow barrier tape around the chair warned that young children might be disturbed by the sight. Another sign said, "Shoplifters will be executed!"

It was all in good Halloween cheer, argued a co-owner of the store, which sold seasonal gifts and novelties.

But the council of churches' director opposed capital punishment, and she was outraged. She mailed a letter to two hundred of her ministerial colleagues, asking that they pressure the store into removing the display.

As a reporter, I drove out to the mall to talk with a few shoppers. One was a fashionably dressed young woman of eighteen.

"I love it. I wish I could buy it," she said, grinning and gazing at the chair. "I'd put it right out in my yard. My little sister loved it when she saw it and she's only seven."

In her letter to local ministers, the council of churches' director had said that "this tawdry 'mock' electric chair panders to the sickest elements in our society that would find such a death 'funny' or 'entertaining.'"

I asked the young customer whether she felt like a sick element.

"I'm not a weirdo freak or anything," she said. "I'm a Baptist."

Basically, the churches' protest didn't get anywhere, even when the Roman Catholic bishop joined in the hue and cry against the chair.

Which cuts to the crux of this whole matter.

On one on side you have well-meaning, highly educated ministers who are bothered by Halloween's history, philosophy, and violent subtexts. On the other side you have millions of children, teenagers, and adults who just want to dress up in weird outfits, eat some candy, and have a little fun.

The twain shall not meet.

This is old news, really. In the Middle Ages, the Roman Catholic Church created All Hallows' Eve on October 31 and All Saints' Day on November 1 specifically to overthrow the occult Samhain festival. It didn't work then. All Hallows' Eve was simply co-opted into the pagan celebration and became the Halloween we celebrate today.

Nevertheless, again today some clergy want us to boycott Halloween. A few churches are trying a variation of what the Catholics did in the Middle Ages—they're attempting to turn a negative into a positive by holding annual "Hallow Him" parties as alternatives to Halloween. There, kids dress up as biblical heroes or angels.

Frankly, we experimented with a few such parties at our own church. Most parents took their kids trick-or-treating first and then brought them to the church party. Which kind of defeated the purpose.

Finally, you have to ask yourself: Is the way we celebrate Halloween any more pagan than the way we celebrate Christmas? Or Easter?

We mark Christmas by sticking up trees inside our houses, dressing fat guys in red suits, and spending bazillions of dollars on Barbie dolls and video games. That captures the essence of Christ's birth, doesn't it? We mark Christianity's holiest event—the raising of Jesus from the dead—with colored eggs and bunny rabbits. Go figure.

The bottom line is that if you give us humans enough time, we'll co-opt anything for our fun and profit. That's one of the thousand or so reasons I believe in original sin.

Yet I don't get too torqued up about our pagan celebrations. You can waste your life fighting one heathenism or another. Even if you win, in the process you often end up creating more abuses yourself, some of them worse than the ones you fought.

So now I largely go with the flow. I occasionally attend a Halloween party. Our church has an Easter egg hunt. I just try to remember that those festivities have little to do with the holy days whose names they bear.

THIS WEEK'S MEDITATION:

"Let me have sense enough to understand the implications of the holidays I celebrate. But let me also have discernment enough to not become a prig or a fanatic."

LOW CHURCH RELIGION
GETS A BAD RAP

My father once took a lengthy break from the pastorate. During that period, my family spent several of my formative years attending a reserved church in a college town, a church where everyone dressed to the nines, where many people left the Sunday services talking more about what the other worshipers had worn than about the preacher's urbane sermons. I admired the pomp, even if the faith itself eluded me back then.

But by 1982, with several stops in between, at age twenty-six and with no training, I paradoxically found myself hired as the reluctant, part-time pastor of a humble little congregation called Pentecostal Grace Tabernacle. It was the church in which my wife had grown up, a Pentecostal group on the wrong side of the tracks. There, people whooped with joy or terror and occasionally spoke in tongues. I came to Pentecostal Grace by accident, I thought—and out of financial necessity, I knew—intending to leave within a few months. I ended up staying fourteen years.

The people at Grace Church, as we eventually came to call it, possessed a radically different view of the world from the folks among whom I'd been reared. I'm ashamed now to say that I initially thought myself superior to my fellow pilgrims there.

Grace Church was a small group when I arrived, perhaps ten families. The men didn't bother to wear ties; maybe they didn't own any. There were a couple of electricians, an auto body repairman, a disabled service station attendant, a laid-off truck driver, a carpenter. The women were housewives mostly and a nurse's aide. Toddlers wandered up and down the aisles at will during the services and no one noticed.

Frequently, the singing was off-key. On one Sunday morning or another, I'd find myself standing near my wife's grandmother, who was named Grace like the church itself. Granny Grace was the widow of a tenant farmer. She kept her long hair braided and wrapped around the back of her head. Sometimes, she wore her flowered house duster to church. If the Spirit happened to hit her just right, and it often did, she'd ball a fist and jerk her arm above her head. "Oh, glory!" she'd shout.

The first time she did that, I nearly fainted.

Slowly, I got where I kind of liked it.

I started to see that the members of Grace Church knew things about God I didn't. They felt His presence in their workplace as clearly as they felt it in the sanctuary. They realized that God had created our emotions as well as our intellects—and that He meant us to use those emotions even in worship. They were more concerned about loving and caring for their neighbors than about the latest theological trend.

I visited other congregations, too, churches that tended to be like ours only more so, where pimply teenagers plucked electric bass guitars as women with beehive hairdos stomped their heels ecstatically on hardwood floors. Singers clapped in time (or some semblance thereof) to camp meeting songs. The preachers' grammar was atrocious, by and large, and they never thought of preparing their sermons in advance. They said, instead, whatever occurred to them, throwing great gobs of spittle out across the pulpit as they built to emotional crescendos.

It was a far cry, literally, from anything I'd known.

Yet today, even though we've since merged Grace Church with my dad's congregation and it exists no more, I'm still living the lessons I absorbed there. Today, every time I visit a sanctuary where everybody is dressed well and talks properly and has good manners, I get a little uncomfortable.

Reading the gospels and Acts in the Bible, I can't help but be startled by the differences between the New Testament church and the great majority of contemporary churches. I'm coming to think that many congregations are far too respectable.

Those earliest Christians bore an aura of earthiness, even a taint of scandal. The president of the local seminary doesn't tend to get crucified between two thieves. Jesus did. And what a mob Jesus' followers were: a pro-Jewish terrorist, a traitorous tax collector who had sold out his fellow Jews for Roman profits, several profane and uneducated fishermen. A company of louts, one commentator has called them. The arguments between the terrorist, Simon the Zealot, and Matthew, the traitorous tax gatherer, must have kept Jesus awake many nights.

Saint Paul, himself an educated and articulate disciple, put the idea bluntly to the church at Corinth: "For you see your calling, brethren," he wrote to them, "that not many wise men after the flesh are called, not many mighty, not many noble."

But Saint Paul wasn't condemning the new Christians. He was praising them.

For "God has chosen the foolish things of the world to confound the wise," he continued. "And God has chosen the weak things of the world to confound the things which are mighty, and the base things of the world, and things which are despised, God has chosen."

God did this, according to Paul, so that no human beings could get puffed up about their own greatness in God's presence. God doesn't need to share His glory with mere people. That would be about like the Queen of England knighting a pompous orangutan. So God instead visits His favor upon the lowly, those who are most clearly undeserving, just to shame and ridicule the self-important. Or that's how Paul saw it.

I don't think that attending a Holy Roller church on the wrong side of the tracks made me or its lifelong members godlier than anybody else. Backwoods churches have as many problems and sins as any other churches. And although uptown churches increasingly make me itchy, I figure God is big enough to embrace the people there, too. I suspect he loves those in thousand-dollar suits as well as those in faded house dusters, as long as they remember that beneath those suits their skin is com-posed of dust.

Still, whenever I recall Granny Grace, her eyes wet with joy, throwing up her fist, raising her lined face toward the ceiling, and shouting, "Oh, glory!"—I'm glad I spent time at that little run-down church.

I keep hoping that a bit of that old woman's glory rubbed off on me.

THIS WEEK'S MEDITATION:

"I won't think more highly of myself than I ought. I'll remember that I share one trait with even the most annoying fundamentalist: We were both created from dirt."

MY "LOST WEEKEND"
GETS FOUND

I was still working full-time as a newspaper reporter. I was finishing a new book, too. I'd just taken the congregation of which I'd long been the part-time pastor, Grace Church, through a merger with my dad's congregation; it had proven to be a stressful and time-consuming endeavor.

I hadn't had any time off in months. My brain was frazzled. So I left one Friday to spend a few days alone at a remote lodge in Ohio. I intended to sit on a breezy balcony, stare at a lake in the woods, and refresh my spirits.

Instead, once there, I fell into an exhausted despair. I decided I was tired of attempting to follow God. I was sick of journalism. My wife had been wonderful to me, but so many years with anybody was too long. By Saturday, I'd resolved to renounce my faith and my call to the ministry. I would quit my newspaper job, too, abandon my family, and move alone to Maine. At forty, I would start a new life.

I even took up smoking cigarettes again, a habit I'd kicked ages ago. Reacquiring that vice was hard, because I'd booked a nonsmoking room. Every time I needed a puff, I had to get in my car and go for a drive. I'd smoke and ride and listen to blue-grass music and feel sorry for myself.

Fortunately, when it came time to return home on Monday, I returned to my senses as well. After crossing the Ohio River back into Kentucky, I tossed my Marlboros out the car window, adding littering to my vacation sins.

I arrived feeling more whipped than when I'd left. However, I'd previously been scheduled to speak at two upcoming services at our church, a Wednesday night meeting and the following Sunday morning service.

It's not wise for a pastor to elaborate on his faults to two congregations that have just tenuously tried to merge into one. But on Wednesday evening I somehow felt compelled to tell what had happened on my trip.

I was nervous. Still, I talked about the disturbing detours my thoughts had taken, about how I'd fallen into old patterns of the mind and the flesh and had nearly dumped everything that matters. I told my fellow churchgoers that I needed their presence, and God's, to keep me rational.

Through the years I've spoken publicly hundreds of times, inside and outside of churches. But I've rarely said anything that hit the nerve this sermon did.

Afterward my listeners laughed and pumped my hand and told me how much they identified with my situation; they'd been there. Others said my words had opened their eyes. One wept and hugged me.

For the rest of the week I considered how strange this was. It occurred to me that God had taken even my glaring weaknesses and had used them for a good end. He'd allowed my parishioners, some of whom I barely knew, to see me, one of their pastors, as a human being. And in my sins they'd witnessed their own. They'd understood that they weren't unusually wicked.

I decided to talk about that paradox in the Sunday morning service.

Here's where it gets weirder. Sunday, as the people sang their praises, bare minutes before I got up to speak, two strangers walked into the sanctuary, hunted seats, and sat down.

I stepped to the podium. Briefly I recapped my lost weekend and what had happened at the Wednesday service.

Then I read aloud a passage from Psalm 139, supposedly written by King David. There were times, David said, when he was so happy he felt as if he'd ascended into heaven—and he'd found God there. But he'd also experienced darker moments when he felt as if he'd fallen into hell. He said that God was in the darkness, too, waiting there to rescue him, waiting to guide him back home.

I talked about how God seems to be constantly redeeming our lives, in the bad moments as well as the good, using our struggles to inspire other unsteady souls.

As I was closing, abruptly one of those two strangers popped to his feet and asked if he could speak. Hesitantly I agreed, shocked but not knowing what else to do. It's rare that a total stranger asks to take over another church's worship service.

The man turned to face the audience. He was a pastor at a

church in a distant region of Kentucky, he announced. He'd gotten burned out. He'd wanted to quit.

At 5:00 A.M. that morning he and his companion, who was a member of his congregation, had fled for eastern Kentucky to find a mutual friend, only to get there and discover their pal had moved. Someone told them the guy might be living in our town, so they'd then driven here. Altogether they'd wandered more than three hundred miles that morning, not knowing where they were going.

They'd passed our rural church's sign, just as they'd passed countless others. But as they went by our sign the pastor had told his companion, who was behind the wheel, to hit the car's brakes and back up. "This is where we're supposed to be," the pastor had said.

They'd hesitated about coming in, he said, because they knew the service had already begun. But no sooner had they entered the building than I had spoken precisely to this preacher's situation.

I'd been burned out; he'd been burned out. I'd run off on a weekend; so had he. I'd wanted to resign my post; he'd wanted to resign his. But God had enabled me to come home. God had turned my bad experience to a good end.

This pastor was convinced God had brought him all those miles just to hear my message. (Why God chose such a circuitous route, he didn't say.) Now he could go home again, he said, reassured the Lord truly was working in his life.

Our newly merged congregation erupted in a spontaneous standing ovation.

Me, I stood there like a sap and grinned.

The longer I endeavor—so feebly—to trust God, the more he amazes me. And the less I know what He'll do next.

THIS WEEK'S MEDITATION:

"Lord, You're always working for my good, even in bad situations. As a minister once said, if my life were drawn as a time line on a sheet of paper, You couldn't be represented by a second line intersecting mine at some crucial point. You're the paper itself— going before me, beyond me, above me, and below me."

WE TRUST IN SATELLITES' BEAMS AND E-MAILS

Even though I'm a minister, sometimes it's difficult for me to trust in matters of the spirit. Let's face it, religion spends a lot of time talking about beings that can't be seen. God, we're told, is a Spirit. Jesus likened Him to air: everywhere at once, inside us and all around us, but invisible. The Bible also implies that our atmosphere is thick with celestial angels and fallen demons going about errands that directly affect our lives.

Christianity, at least, tells us that the invisible frequently is more real than the visible. Jesus put it like this: "Blessed are those who have not seen, and yet believe." It tells us that God, even on His most foolish day, is more brilliant than the wisest human.

Periodically I have a hard time grasping all that. I want to believe in things I can see with my eyes, grasp with my hands, and understand with my own limited brain. I used to go to places such as New York City and see the throngs—all colors, all shapes, all religions—and I'd wonder: "How could God possibly know me among all these people? How could He hear my silent prayers? How could He care about me as an individual?"

When I really think about it, though, I realize that even in our natural, daily existence, there probably are as many real and powerful things we can't see, and don't understand, as things we do:

- You can't see atoms. But after scientists isolated them in a laboratory and split them, atoms unleashed mighty explosions capable of destroying whole civilizations.

- A seminary professor once told me a story, perhaps apocryphal, about a fuel-company manager who was sent to investigate a rash of work-related deaths. Supposedly empty gas barrels were killing employees. The barrels had been declared safe, but every time a worker lit a cigarette lighter to peer inside one, it blew him to kingdom come. The secret, of course, was that the barrels still contained gas fumes. The barrels looked empty, but looks were deceiving.

- You can't see germs with the naked eye. But doctors say half of all colds could be prevented if people would scrub their hands frequently, washing away those microscopic agents of sickness.

While we're at it, consider as well these marvels of communications and science that, although developed by humans, defy explanation for most of us:

- An explorer in New Zealand or the jungles of Africa can send e-mail—without speaking a word—halfway around the earth to his wife in the United States. His wife can read the message and respond in seconds, without anyone else hearing. Magically, computer systems in distant countries sort out these loving correspondents from the tens of millions of other people using similar computers and direct the spouses' notes to their intended targets.

· I can feed into a computer search engine three or four basic words contained anywhere in the text of any single newspaper story published in the last fifteen years by any major paper in the United States. The full story then appears on my home computer's screen. I don't need to know beforehand the story's author, its headline, or the date on which it appeared.

· A friend of mine owns a home theater system that's fed by a large-dish satellite in his yard. He can tap buttons on the remote control in his living room in Kentucky and instantly pull down live programs from Japan or the Sudan. His remote control somehow bounces an invisible signal to the satellite dish in his yard, which beams another signal to a satellite orbiting the earth. The space satellite selects an invisible beam from, say, Japan, reroutes it to my pal's dish and then to his large-screen TV. All this happens faster than it took you to read this paragraph. My buddy tells me, by the way, that each of us humans constantly is surrounded and even pierced by waves from satellites, radios, and cellular phones that are passing information through the air.

- A skilled researcher can punch a few computer buttons and find out a stranger's name, address, phone number, employer, income, and credit history. She can determine who the person's next-door neighbors are and how much they make, and the names and addresses of the businesses closest to the stranger's house. The computer will draw a map from the researcher's office to the stranger's front door.

- You and I can insert a videotaped biography of a celebrity into a VCR and review the beginning, middle, or end of her life at will. The movie star may be long dead, but we can hear her speak and see her move as if she were alive right now.

- In 1995 the Reverend Billy Graham preached to one billion people in 185 countries in 117 different languages all at one moment, by satellite from San Juan.

- From a drop of your blood, a geneticist can determine who your parents were, what diseases they carried, and whether you've inherited those same ills.

If the minds of humans produced these wonders, aren't we silly to think that the Creator of the universe can't hear us when we pray silently? That He can't sort out our messages from those of other people? That He can't find us in a crowd—or in a jungle?

Why wouldn't He know the stories of our lives, where we've come from, and where we're going? Why wouldn't He understand our sicknesses and be able to heal them?

He is, after all, God.

THIS WEEK'S MEDITATION:

"Lord, we always say, 'Seeing is believing.' You tell us, 'Believe first, and then you'll see.' We get the order backward. Help me to set it right in my life."

GOD'S FAVOR CAN
OPEN DOORS

In 1984, I was nearly at my wit's end. I'd earlier returned to the University of Kentucky to finish my degree and learn to be a writer. I'd completed my bachelor's degree in English in 1982, at the ripe age of twenty-six, but still didn't know enough about my craft to make a living at it. So I'd pressed on, into UK's master's degree program in English.

To help support my wife and me during my grad-school days, I'd done a lot of things, including working as a university teaching assistant, delivering newspapers daily on a rural route, and pastoring a tiny church. Renee was a bank clerk, but earned little.

While I was laboring toward my master's degree, Renee delivered our son. After completing her unpaid maternity leave, she'd cut back her bank schedule so she could spend more time with our new baby.

By the spring of 1984, as I finished my master's in English, we were broke. I had an infant to feed and a wife who was working only part-time. I'd won acceptance to a prestigious program in creative writing at the University of Virginia, but was forced to turn down the offer because we couldn't afford to move.

I still had no prospects for any kind of full-time career as a writer, or for any other full-time job. The country was, as I recall, in a deep recession. At least I was in a deep recession. It seemed that every door I tried to open was locked.

I kept trying to solve my problems myself. I talked with a military science recruiter at UK about the possibility of joining the army, maybe in an officer-training program. I thought about going to UK's law school, but didn't know how I'd pay my way through three years of intensive study there, given that the law school didn't even offer the meager supplement of teaching assistantships. I thought about selling insurance. I thought about earning yet another master's degree, in journalism, to get the kind of hands-on experience that might enable me to land a gig at a newspaper or magazine. Heck, I thought about almost everything, including jumping off a bridge.

Then one night I was flipping through *The Living Bible*, a paraphrase of the Scriptures in contemporary language. I happened across a verse in Proverbs that said something like this: "A man flips a coin, but God decides which side comes up."

I remembered that in the Acts of the Apostles, when the eleven remaining disciples were looking for a new twelfth man to replace Judas Iscariot, they had cast lots to identify the one God had chosen.

On an impulse, figuring I had nothing to lose, I wrote down on individual slips of paper each of the eight or ten options I was considering. After folding the slips I dropped them into a hat, shook the hat vigorously, and tossed the papers onto the carpet.

I prayed silently for God's hand to lead mine. Then I drew a slip of paper and unfolded it. "College of Communications," it said.

The College of Communications at UK included the university's School of Journalism. That's what I'd written to indicate the option of pursuing journalistic training.

The next day I made an appointment to talk with the communications college's director of graduate studies.

I arrived in his office feeling sheepish. He didn't know me, and I wasn't about to admit I'd chosen his program by drawing it from a hat. I just said I wanted to enroll as a master's degree student, mainly to study journalism. I knew I'd missed the deadline for applying for a teaching assistantship, I said, but I badly needed work.

"Well," he said, "the head of the journalism school has an opening for a graduate assistant. It's the only job we have left in the college. He's interviewed some people but hasn't picked anybody. Do you have time to talk with him?"

"You bet," I said.

Within minutes I was sitting in the office of the then director of journalism, a nationally recognized scholar and former Washington, D.C., reporter named Ed Lambeth.

He hired me on the spot.

Not long afterward, I learned that I'd also won a high-paying internship at IBM for which a professor in my old English department had recommended me.

Suddenly I had not one but three paying positions—as a graduate assistant, an IBM technical writer, and a part-time pastor. I found myself earning eight hundred dollars a week, a considerable sum for a graduate student in 1984.

But a greater boon followed. As I studied and worked in the journalism school, I formed friendships with Lambeth and other professors there. They became dedicated mentors to me, simply from their kind hearts. Lambeth, I learned, could make one call and secure me any fellowship or internship I wanted.

Everything good that's happened to me since as a writer—including an internship at the *Lexington Herald-Leader* that led to my first full-time job as a journalist—grew directly from that one fateful night when I threw a few slips of paper on the carpet of our cramped apartment.

There's a term in the Christian faith for that kind of blessing. It's called favor. It means that, if we're making any serious attempt at all to be obedient to God, we can expect His undeserved intervention in our lives. From time to time He simply gives us gifts.

We're to work and do the best we can, of course. But often our best isn't enough.

That's when God takes over.

THIS WEEK'S MEDITATION:

"Lord, help me believe these words You spoke through a wise man many years ago: 'Do not forget My teaching, but let your heart keep My commandments. . . . So shall you find favor and a good name in the sight of God and man. Trust in the Lord with all your heart, and lean not to your own understanding. In all your ways acknowledge Him, and He shall direct your paths.'"

THIS IS THE SEASON TO
COUNT YOUR BLESSINGS

Every autumn I find myself humming "Count Your Blessings," a hymn from my days as a Baptist youth. I guess my brain veers off on one of those spontaneous neurological detours it's wont to take more and more as I age, transporting me from one era of my life to another.

During this season, as the whole nation annually observes the giving of thanks, I do just what the hymn suggests: enumerate the blessings I've received.

It's not an original idea, I realize. Nevertheless, here goes:

I'm thankful for my wife and our child, both of whom seem to love me more than I have a right to expect. (I do grow weary of people telling me that Renee is an infinitely better-looking woman than I am a man.)

I'm thankful for parents who have lived such exemplary Christian lives that, no matter how far I've wandered spiritually, I've always known there's such a thing as genuine faith.

I'm thankful for my sister, who has overcome a divorce and a single mother's financial hardships to continue her education and bring up a smart, happy son.

I'm thankful for my new brother-in-law, a towering four-hundred-pound ex-wrestler turned deputy sheriff. He's not your typical brother-in-law, but he's brought a joy and peace back to my sister's face I never thought I'd see again.

I'm thankful for my wife's huge brood of relatives, all of whom live nearby. Well, usually I'm thankful for them.

I'm thankful for our church, which has taught me that emotional, joyous worship has its place.

I'm thankful for my late grandparents.

I'm thankful for the Spirit.

I'm thankful for my job.

I'm thankful for good health.

I'm thankful for farmers. They're probably the most important people in society—want to try surviving without them?—and the least appreciated.

I'm thankful for my shiny black sports car. Despite what my wife tells our friends, I don't drive it because I'm having a midlife crisis. I simply like sleek, fast cars and always have. Everybody needs a few vices. That's one of mine.

I'm thankful for a restaurant in Lexington called the Parkette Drive In. It's an anachronism, having survived virtually unchanged since the 1950s, complete with curb service. Somebody in that venerable hamburger stand churns up the best butterscotch milkshakes on the planet.

I'm thankful for football.

I'm thankful for the few politicians from across the spectrum—wacky liberals to right-wing zealots—who stand up staunchly for what they believe is correct and take the resulting criticism. A waffler by nature, I'm inspired by people with spines, even when I think their views are wrong.

I'm thankful for Ale-8-One, a ginger ale–like regional soft drink that's bottled just a few miles up the highway from where I live.

I'm thankful for books and the eyesight to read them.

I'm thankful for the Bible.

I'm thankful for the sitting room at our house, with its floor-to-ceiling bookshelves, leather wingback chairs, and cozy fireplace.

I'm thankful to have a little money in the bank.

I'm thankful for movies, VCRs, and cable TV, especially the Arts & Entertainment Channel's *Biography* documentaries and the History Channel's war documentaries.

I'm thankful for the geniuses who cranked out marvelous script after marvelous script for all those great old television series: *The Andy Griffith Show*, *The Dick Van Dyke Show*, *Taxi*, *Cheers*, *Hill Street Blues*, and *All in the Family*. I can't count the hours of pleasure these shows have brought me.

I'm thankful for democracy.

I'm thankful for Bob Seger, John Prine, Merle Haggard, and Miles Davis. Roughly forty years after he began work on it, Davis's classic album *Kind of Blue* still sounds to me like a work of God.

I'm thankful for my friends—and for the range of their experiences. Some are agnostics and some are ministers; some are factory workers and some are professors; some are ex-cops and some are ex-cons. All have taught me things I otherwise wouldn't have known.

I'm thankful for the people who criticize me, who force me to reexamine myself. But I'm less thankful for them than for my pals.

I'm thankful for the year and a half my wife, my son, and I got to spend with our boxer, Max, before he was tragically hit by a truck. We'd never known before that it was possible to love a dog as dearly as a human member of the family.

I'm thankful for electricity, air-conditioning, central heating, and indoor plumbing.

I'm thankful for home computers, copiers, fax machines, and cellular phones.

I'm thankful for the rare, quiet days when I don't have to use any of those gadgets I just mentioned.

I'm thankful for king-size beds and for being able to sleep late in mine on Saturdays.

I'm thankful that my family and I are able to take annual vacations to interesting sites such as New York City or Las Vegas. But I'm always more glad to get home than I was to go.

I'm thankful for all three of my college degrees, difficult as they were to earn and little as they've benefited me financially.

I'm thankful for the hard times I've endured, because they left me stronger than I otherwise would have been. But I don't want to endure them again.

I'm thankful for life.

I'm thankful that I'm not afraid of death, in theory at least.

I'm thankful for the promise of life after death, even if I can't prove it's true.

THIS WEEK'S MEDITATION:

"Help me count my blessings rather than curse my troubles. For in doing so I'll be happier—and more pleasant to others."

48 Week

HE CARES ABOUT
THE NEUROTIC

The biggest increase in my prayer life started, I think, when I became a father. Nothing will drop you to your knees as quickly as parenthood. Before my son was born I'd always assumed that, as adults took possession of their first child at the hospital, nature imbued them with wisdom for the great task ahead of them. Then Renee and I brought John home and immediately I discovered I was just as dim-witted as ever.

Many times in the past fifteen years I've called on God with a fervor to which childless men and women probably can't relate.

One such episode was when John, then eleven, prepared to attend public school for the first time. Years earlier, just before he started kindergarten, Renee and I had been greatly impressed by a child we knew who had just completed kindergarten at a private, church-run school in our town.

So we enrolled our son at the same school. We were so tickled with the results that we kept him there through first grade. Then through second grade. And so on right up through fifth grade, which is as far as the Christian school here goes.

Our son's class was small, made up of polite children and dedicated, religious teachers. We hoped to find a way for him to somehow continue in a private school.

It wasn't meant to be.

Despite our druthers, he entered sixth grade at our town's large public middle school. All three of us had heard horror stories about public schools: that older students often beat up younger ones, that the curriculum was confused, that the teachers were uncaring. It was the most dramatic change John had ever faced.

Then, in church the Sunday before public school classes were to start, someone suggested that the congregation pray for all the children present who were about to begin their new school year. The congregation's children, including John, joined hands at the front of the sanctuary. As the pastor, I led the prayer. As a father, I just about climbed Jacob's ladder into heaven itself, I was beseeching the Almighty so intensely.

However, by that Tuesday, the day before classes began, we'd forgotten our faith. I drove my son to Lexington for a last jaunt of movies and laser tag. It wasn't much fun. He was nearly witless with school dread.

That same night, our family attended an open house for new middle school students. We met our son's homeroom teacher. She had been my wife's teacher when Renee was in the sixth grade! Seeing each other again, they hit it off big-time.

I also learned that the teacher and I shared a close mutual friend.

Another child asked the teacher meekly whether the eighth graders picked on the sixth graders.

"If anyone threatens you the least bit," she warned her students, "just tell the nearest teacher. We will stop it. We do not tolerate bullying here. Ever."

We met other faculty members, all of whom seemed similarly nice and caring.

John stopped by the sign-up table for students interested in joining the school band. The band director, it turned out, was the father of one of his friends from the Christian school.

The evening developed into one of those rare times when everything that can go well goes even better. By the time we returned home, John was so joyful he couldn't sleep.

By Friday, the third day of classes, he told me he liked his new school even better than his old one.

I know: All this might have been just a pleasant coincidence. But it felt like an answer to our supplications. "Thank you, Lord," I whispered.

John got that same feeling. One evening soon after, he chattered happily about his band class. He'd already known how to play the drums quite well.

But the band director had announced that too many kids wanted to beat the limited number of drum sets; the drummer wannabes would all have to take a musical test. Some would need to learn the trombone or tuba instead.

"Dad, let's pray that I'll get to stay on the drums," John said.

"We can pray for that if you'd like," I said. "But maybe God's smarter than we are. Let's ask that He'll lead you to the instrument that's best for you, drums or not."

He considered that.

"Yeah," he said. "Let's pray for Him to lead me. That's better."

I'm not sure whether my suggestion was the result of wisdom—or whether I just didn't have enough faith to specifically ask the Lord to let John to play the drums. Nevertheless, we prayed.

He got the drums.

Now that John's a teenager, faring well in a public high school, I can see that we all overreacted to his first days in the local middle school. It wasn't as if he was entering Alcatraz. And in the long run it probably didn't matter whether he was chosen to play the drums in the sixth-grade band; he had a set of drums at home to play and another at church.

But I'm reminded, too, that Jesus said God cares about the tiniest matters affecting His creation—the number of hairs on our heads, the deaths of sparrows, the blooming of lilies. I think, well, maybe He also cares about eleven-year-old boys who need encouragement, and their overprotective parents.

THIS WEEK'S MEDITATION:

"Lord, help me to see You as the God of the small things as well as the large. Let me trust You in both."

49 Week

THE WALL BETWEEN LIFE
AND DEATH IS THIN

Recently I helped officiate at the funeral of a thirty-seven-year-old man, the father of a teenage girl about my son's age. He collapsed one evening at an auto auction. By the next morning he was dead from an aneurysm he hadn't known was there.

Within days, a twenty-one-year-old University of Kentucky football player was driving two friends on a deer-hunting trip. Their pickup veered off the road and flipped, injuring the driver badly and killing both his buddies. As I write this, the kid at the wheel has been charged with drunken driving and two counts of second-degree manslaughter. Whether or not he's convicted, certainly his life has been shattered.

Once, when I was a senior in high school, three friends and I skipped classes and headed for the next county to buy beer. Then we drove around all afternoon drinking ourselves into oblivion, mostly confining our itinerary to crooked one-lane country roads so we could avoid cops.

The driver, drunk as a lord, started speeding. We popped over a hill and found a cement truck parked horizontally across the road, blocking our path.

We were traveling sixty miles an hour when we hit it.

Our car ricocheted off the truck, careened up an embankment, hurtled across a yard, flew downward over a second embankment, and passed through a stand of trees.

We came to rest on the same road we'd been knocked off of—around the next curve. Our car was totaled. All four of us guys walked away unscratched.

I've come similarly close to dying or suffering disabling injuries well over a dozen times that I know of, in several car wrecks, in a horseback-riding accident, by violence, in a near fall from a high bridge, twice by almost drowning, twice by narrowly escaping electrocution.

I'm still here and still standing, and I don't know why, really.

As I mentioned earlier in this book, I nearly died before I was born. By the time I'd struggled down my mother's birth canal and finally poked my head into the bright light of this world, my skull was mashed grotesquely.

This happened in small-town Kentucky in 1956. There were no medical specialists available to negotiate such emergencies. The general practitioner who presided over my delivery simply said to my mother, as they regarded my temporarily misshapen head, "John Henry had a hard time."

My brother wasn't as lucky. By 1960, we had moved to another little Kentucky town. Again my mom went into labor, and again the birth proved treacherous. My mom was unable to deliver this baby at all. The young doctor attending her waited too long to perform an emergency cesarean section.

My brother—his name was Timothy Edward—smothered in our mom's womb. Otherwise, he was a flawless infant, a fat, pretty baby. In the funeral home, I touched his tiny fingers, and asked my dad why the baby's hand was so cold.

Mom never became pregnant again; the doctor said it would be too dangerous for her and the fetus. My sister later came to us through adoption. So you might say that my parents' biological children had a fifty-fifty chance of surviving birth.

It wouldn't occur to me for decades to ask God, or myself, or the wind, why I'd lived and Timothy hadn't. It could so easily have been the other way around.

When I was about twelve, I was riding my pony Duke alone on an isolated farm. I sat in a new saddle of which I was immensely proud. For some reason, though I knew Duke didn't like to wade through water, I decided to take him across a shallow pond.

Halfway across, Duke stopped. He tossed his head, his eyes wild. He thrashed the water with his front hooves. He buckled his knees as if he intended to lie down and wallow. I jerked the reins. I kicked his ribs. I whacked his rump with a switch. Nothing helped.

We started to fall. My reflex was to jump, but I remembered my prized saddle and stayed on, yelling at the pony, trying desperately to keep him upright.

Then I was submerged, Duke's full weight on top of me. Filthy pond water shot up my nose. My feet were still in the stirrups. Had the pond's bottom been rocky, I likely would have been crushed. But the bottom was made of gooey mud, and I sank in it.

I'd sometimes seen Duke roll at the pond's edge when I wasn't riding him. Typically he'd lie on his back and writhe from side to side. In the black water, I realized he might do that with me beneath him. If he had, I might have drowned.

He didn't. He rolled across me, climbed to his feet, and galloped away, the reins flopping. I popped to the surface scared, wet, and muddy, but otherwise okay.

You might say this accident wasn't so serious. But I've known people who died under lesser circumstances. My wife's sixteen-year-old cousin was cutting firewood. His chain saw ran out of gas, so he carried it into his house's unfinished basement. He unscrewed the caps on the saw and on a gasoline can, then apparently flipped on a light switch to better see what he was doing. The switch had an electrical short and threw out a spark. The spark ignited the gas fumes. The gas can exploded and gruesomely burned the boy to death in his own basement, on a beautiful spring afternoon.

How do you determine why some people die early and others live on?

You can agonize over it, but there isn't any clear explanation. That's just how the cosmos works. Maybe it's predestination. Maybe I've been spared because of the prayers of my long-suffering parents. Maybe it's all plain, dumb luck. Ask me on five successive days and I'll give you five different answers.

But this much I've learned for sure: There are few guarantees for any of us. The wall that separates us from the hereafter is thinner than a communion wafer. We each should be prepared to break through it at any moment.

This week's meditation:

"God, I'm so grateful for Your protection thus far. But since I don't know the day on which I might depart this life, help me stay ready to meet You face to face with no advance notice."

RELIGIOUS REVIVALS OFFER
HOPE FOR OUR WORLD

Most politicians—and journalists—keep missing what someday will prove to have been the major social revolution of our time: a convulsion of spontaneous Christian revivals that increasingly have been sweeping the globe since at least the early 1900s.

After I left my full-time newspaper job in 1997 to become a full-time minister, a smaller, briefer one of these unscheduled events broke out at the church on the cusp of Appalachia that I now copastor with my father.

A businessman who then was part of our congregation was speaking from the pulpit in a regular Sunday evening service when the glory of God just fell on the church. We came back the next night to see if God's tangible presence would visit us again. It did, so we came back the next night, too. And the next. We saw visitors converted, sick people healed. We weren't used to this kind of thing, but there it was.

By the following Sunday, the sanctuary was packed to capacity with worshipers who had heard of the meetings by word of mouth. We hadn't advertised. We had no idea what to advertise.

Our visitation from the Almighty, for want of a better explanation, lasted only about a week. But I learned something from watching people's reaction to it. Here and everywhere, folks simply are starving for God's presence.

What we experienced is only a minuscule ripple in a spiritual sea change that is flooding the world. Scholars say that, taken together, these innumerable, spontaneous outbreaks make up the most momentous development in Christianity since the Protestant Reformation of the 1500s. The implications for governments and societies are enormous.

This worldwide revivalistic fervor can be traced directly to the rise of Pentecostalism, a branch of Christianity that's grown from less than 1 percent of all Christians in the early 1900s to 500 million adherents today, or as much as a quarter of all Christians. *Charisma* magazine has cited one study predicting that if current trends continue, there will be 1.14 billion Pentecostals by 2025.

Pentecostals teach that it's possible for contemporary Christians to experience God's power firsthand just as the earliest Christians did. They prophesy, exorcise demons, collapse under the power of God.

In South Korea, a nation once considered impenetrable by missionaries, 40 percent of the people have embraced Christianity; nearly all are Pentecostals. In the People's Republic of China, a Communist state, between 30 million and 100 million people have converted. In England, 68 percent of Anglicans and 80 percent of Baptists say they have taken part in such Pentecostal "gifts of the Spirit" as healing and supernatural "words of knowledge."

In 1994, a huge, Pentecostal-style revival spontaneously broke out at Toronto's Airport Vineyard church. It has lasted ever since and has drawn hundreds of thousands of visitors from virtually every continent—so many that *Toronto Life* magazine labeled the "Toronto Blessing" the city's number one tourist attraction. That revival has spread worldwide into churches of all stripes.

A similar revival began later at the Brownsville Assembly of God in Pensacola, Florida. For years, thousands have lined up early in the day to get a seat for nightly services. Tens of thousands have been converted there.

As I said, the implications are enormous. Let me point out two.

First, globally, hundreds of millions of people apparently have found little in governments or commerce that satisfies the longing of their hearts. They're turning inward, seeking meaning in personal, emotional relationships with God.

A friend of mine lamented that these Christians are using religion as a selfish justification for burying their heads in the sand.

If so, that will soon change—which leads me to a second implication of this phenomenon. Previous mass revivals rarely have remained personal and private for long. Historically, once the initial ecstasy passed, many whose hearts had been warmed (to lift a phrase from the Methodist revivalist John Wesley) shifted their attentions outward, toward reforming public society.

Today's social moderates and liberals, eyeballing such groups as the ultraconservative Christian Coalition, might cringe at such a thought. But they shouldn't. While Muslim revivals in the Middle East have led to state takeovers by rigid fundamentalists, for whatever reasons that doesn't seem to have been the case with Christian revivals.

The Dark Ages and the Inquisition weren't the works of Christians who had been revived, but those whose faith had turned overly legalistic and hostile to such spiritual renewals. To the contrary, men and women who recently have been converted or refreshed by an encounter with the Spirit tend to feel they should extend the compassion of Jesus to others.

Grassroots Christian revivals in America and England, such as the First and Second Great Awakenings, resulted in the most progressive of political and social changes. Revivalists and their converts led public fights to build orphanages, establish public schools, outlaw child labor, and end slavery.

A key problem with government as we now have it, I think, is that well-meaning politicians on the right and left think they can best impose reforms from the top down, by simply passing new laws. That proves exceedingly difficult. Politicians and their constituents grow disillusioned and cynical.

Legislation alone, you see, can temporarily alter people's behaviors, but rarely changes their minds. Laws can briefly force a racist to stop acting like a racist, but they can't make him quit thinking like one. Eventually, when an opportunity arises, he'll burn crosses again.

Revivalists know that true, lasting societal change has to start in individual hearts. And only God, not politicians, can transform hearts.

THIS WEEK'S MEDITATION:

"Lord, as the hymn writer said, please send a revival—and let it begin with me. Assign Your Spirit to quicken me with a renewed faith and an impassioned love for You and my fellow humans. Teach me to care about the addicted and the unhappy. Let me know from experience how real You are. Feed my soul."

WE SHOULD
REMEMBER GRACE

During my years as a journalist, I dealt with religious people of every imaginable hue: Presbyterians and Pentecostals, Baptists and Buddhists, Calvinists and Catholics, Methodists and Muslims, Jews and Jehovah's Witnesses.

Frequently my experiences among these folks proved uncommonly pleasant. Within every faith I met people of genuine goodness, generosity, and mercy.

But some of my forays among the godly weren't happy at all.

I learned that religion, used wrongly, can bring out the worst in humanity.

Once I got a call from a conservative Baptist minister. Lest you think I'm about to single out Baptists for a bad-mouthing, let me point out again that I was raised among several generations of Baptists whom I loved.

But none of that got me anywhere with this guy, who had called me at my desk in the newsroom. I couldn't possibly be a "real" Christian, he announced matter-of-factly. I'd written a column in which I'd questioned some of the Reverend Jerry Falwell's views. A born-again man of God would never have done that, this pastor assured me.

Oh?

Nope, he said. Besides, I was working for a secular daily newspaper. Nobody who knows the Lord could in good conscience work for the secular media. And in my weekly column I hardly ever railed against abortion, which the Bible says is murder—at least according to my partner in conversation.

I explained that I didn't like abortion either but that, for my life, I couldn't find a word in my Bible about its being murder. I'd looked.

Exactly, the preacher said. My lack of scriptural discernment was proof that I was a heathen.

Trying to remain calm, I reminded this guy that what I could find in my Bible, if memory served me, were verses saying that the only one qualified to judge someone else's soul was God. (Romans 14.) Was this God with whom I was speaking?

No, he said glibly. He wasn't God, but true Christians such as he could judge people like me by our fruits.

Oh, so you're a fruit inspector, I said.

Yes indeed, he replied.

My fruit, apparently, was wormy. He said I'd better give my heart to the Lord and get saved before it was too late—not that he thought I would.

Later, I couldn't decide which annoyed me more: that this servant of the Lord was so certain I was destined for a fiery, torturous hell, or that he seemed so darned happy about it. But by then I'd grown used to such conversations. Over the years I've been consigned to perdition by the best of them, liberals and conservatives.

If these conversations serve no other purpose, they do force me to ask myself, What does it mean to try to live as a serious believer in God?

I'm a churchgoer, even an ordained minister myself. I've been faithfully married for twenty years. My wife leads the music at our church. We pray together a lot. I don't beat our kid. I pay my taxes. I tithe. I don't take dope. I don't drive drunk. I haven't been in a fistfight for a quarter century. I strive, with mixed success, to treat others as I want to be treated.

Evidently none of this matters. I'm doomed because (take your pick here) I: attend boxing matches, watch *Beavis and Butt-Head*, listen to country and rock music, doubt that a few of the stories in the Bible are literally true, think that most of the Bible stories are true, believe that preachers ought not become political demagogues, don't weep over the vanishing rain forest, didn't ask a mentally disturbed homeless man I met to move in with my family.

I'd agree that some of my behavior probably is damnable. After all, I'm human. Does that mean I'm of no account at all? I hope not.

This much I can tell you:

I was reared in a fine Christian home. But as a teenager I rebelled, which isn't unusual for preachers' kids. Even so, during my freshman year in college I attended a conservative religious school. Most of that time I was in serious emotional pain. I was separated from my parents. My best friends had chosen another college. My girlfriend and I had broken up. I drank.

The godly folks at this Christian college showed me no compassion at all. They condemned and disciplined and ostracized me with the same pompous glee I heard in that minister's voice over the phone two decades later. All in the name of Jesus, naturally.

In nine short months, this Christian college managed to turn me from a reasonably religious, if misguided, teenage boy who had been reared in church into an atheist.

I figured that if what these folks had was Christianity, I'd avoid catching it.

Fortunately, years later, I stumbled into a little prayer group of other believers.

I was still messed up. But these Christians did something amazing. They welcomed me . . . just as I was.

They didn't browbeat me. They told me that God loved me even more than they did. They told me they were all sinners, too, clinging to God's grace. They didn't claim to know all the answers about religion or life or sin.

But obviously they knew the most important one. They knew that, as the Good Book says, "Love overcomes a multitude of sins."

By simply loving and accepting me, they saved my life and they changed it. They made a disciple out of me again. Not a perfect Christian, I know. But not the fellow I otherwise would have become either.

245

In the perennial religious battle between grace and legalism, between acceptance and condemnation, I'll put my money on grace every time.

THIS WEEK'S MEDITATION:

"Lord, give me a revelation of Your grace. Let me receive it for myself as divine truth, and let me manifest it toward others."

A REMEMBRANCE OF A
SMALL BOY'S HERO

The floor I sat on was cold. The only heat in the house was from
the coal-burning fireplaces in each room. Closer to one of the
grates, you could toast your legs bright red. But over by the
Christmas tree in the living room, where I was lugging a package
from beneath the spruce, you could almost see your breath.

My maternal grandfather, Oscar Chestnut, sat in a ladder-
back chair, one of his everpresent Camel cigarettes between his
fingers, his legs crossed at the knees.

He smiled, watching me.

I untaped and unfolded the green-and-white wrapping
paper, which my frugal grandmother saved and reused.

And there it was, a Fort Apache action set from Sears, including a plastic-log fort, a tin headquarters building, and molded
plastic soldiers, Indians, and horses.

I'd known for weeks what my gift would be. Every fall, Papa
sat me down on his creaky couch and opened a new Sears Wish
Book on my lap. He'd unfold his reading glasses, then drape a
thick farmer's wrist over my neck.

247

"Okay, Sputnik," he'd say. "Let's see what we can find here."

He called me Sputnik after the first Soviet spaceship. Like the spacecraft, he said, I went around and around.

Papa always told me I could pick out any one toy in the catalog, a mind-boggling opportunity. But even then I perceived that his resources were slim. He farmed forty hilly acres in southeastern Kentucky. He had broken his health trying to till crops from an inch of soil and a foot of shale. Papa had an ulcer, a hernia, and a limp arm.

So I tried to choose toys that wouldn't cost a lot. This particular year, I secretly had lusted after the deluxe Fort Apache set, which contained scores more soldiers, Indians, and accessories. I'd asked, instead, for the smaller version, which was priced several dollars cheaper.

Over weeks of anticipation, though, I'd memorized the dimensions of the toy fort. I knew exactly the number of soldiers, Indians, and horses I would get. I broke open the cardboard box, dumped out the little figures, and began avidly counting, making sure Sears hadn't shorted me. There were scads of them.

"Papa," I said, after a quick tally, "this is the deluxe set!"

"Eh law," he said, rubbing his bald head in feigned confusion. "I must've got my order mixed up."

Then he winked.

❖

Oscar Chestnut wasn't a famous man. He talked with a drawl and a hillbilly's grammar. Mostly he wore bib overalls and brogans. But if I ever had a hero, he was it. I used to rub my palms on fence posts to make them callused like his. I wanted to be like him; I still do.

I didn't love him because he was my grandfather. I've had many relatives I didn't admire. I loved him because of who he was.

In the rural community where he grew up, the two-room school only went to eighth grade. He begged his mother to send him to town to high school. She refused: He didn't need schooling to work on the farm, she said. So he repeated the eighth grade because he liked learning so much.

He also liked gadgets. In the 1940s, before his community was wired by the RECC, he created electricity for his house by rigging up his own generator made of car batteries. In the winters, he sat nights out in an unheated shed, building crude radios from a pile of scattered fuses and wires, until his fingers stiffened with cold.

Papa had as consistent a sense of humor as anybody I knew.

In the 1960s CBS gave us *Green Acres*, the sitcom about a New York lawyer who decides to become a small-time farmer. A genuine hardscrabble farmer himself, Papa found the show amusing, and we used to watch it together when I visited him. He nicknamed my pony "Lisa" after the socialite-turned-farmwife played by Eva Gabor. Papa called his ne'er-do-well beagle "Oliver" after the lawyer, played by Eddie Albert, who weekly proved himself an astonishingly inept man of the soil.

Papa read a lot, and he told marvelous stories. He supplied me with details of America's various wars. He talked about his father, who had spent a youthful decade as a Montana cowboy.

When I was older, I heard city people marvel at Papa. If you bought potatoes from other farmers, it was said, they would load tiny bruised potatoes in the bottom of the bushel basket, then cover those with fat, healthy potatoes to deceive you. When you bought potatoes from Mr. Chestnut, people said, he heaped big potatoes on both the bottom and the top, and kept the small ones for his own supper.

That's who he was. He wasn't a saint. He had a temper and he could cuss like a Texas truck driver. He was sporadic in his church attendance. But he never gave folks a little when he could give much.

❖

In 1968, when I was twelve, one of his arteries burst. He collapsed in his driveway, fifty yards from the log house where he was born.

At his funeral, the church was packed. Leather-faced men, whom I'd never seen demonstrate an ounce of tenderness, wept as if their hearts were shattered.

Nearly twenty years after, among a few of those same men, someone told a funny tale. We laughed until our jaws hurt.

"My stars," one fellow said. "I wish Oscar Chestnut was here."

❖

Renee, who is generous to a fault, gets mildly perturbed with me each Christmas. We have only one child, and we overspend on him anyway. Then, when we've finished all our shopping, I always buy him something extra. During one recent Christmas season we also gave toys and clothes to the kids at an Appalachian children's home. Renee was eager to help. But she said I went overboard. She thinks I get carried away by the season.

Actually, that's not true. It's just something I learned as a child: Never buy the smaller gift when you can give the deluxe. You might say it's the Fort Apache approach to Christmas. It's my way of paying homage to a hero.

THIS WEEK'S MEDITATION:

"I know that in this world there are givers and there are takers. Help me to become one of the givers. Let me be the kind of person of whom those who know me best will say, twenty years after I'm gone, 'My stars. I wish he was here.'"